Just Right

Jeremy Harmer

Grammar materials co-author: Hester Lott

Workbook

ELT Marshall Cavendish London • Singapore • New York

Photo acknowledgements

p5 top l-r: Russ Widstrand/Alamy, ImageState/Alamy, Lightroom Photos/Alamy, Brand X Pictures/Alamy, bottom l-r: Brand X Pictures/Alamy, Tom Tracy Photography/Alamy, Stock Connection, Inc/Alamy, Stock Connection, Inc/Alamy, Goodshot/Alamy, image100/Alamy; p14 Andi Duff/Alamy; p18 Argus, Brighton/Richard Grange; p21 Royalty Free/Corbis; p23 Corbis; p27 Topham Picturepoint; p28 geogphotos/Alamy; p29 David Hoffman Photo Library/Alamy; p32 Penguin Books; p32 Gabe Palmer/Corbis; P42 Hulton-Deutsch Collection/Corbis; p35 MC Archive; p32 Corbis top centre and centre left; p36 Getty Images; p45 Henry VIII, Marshall Cavendish Archive, p45 Portrait of Ann Boleyn(1507-36), Second wife of Henry VIII of England, 1534 by English School (16th century) Hever Castle Ltd, Kent, UK/Bridgeman Art Library; p45 Anne of Cleves (1515-57) AKG London/Eric Lessing; p45 Catherine of Aragon (1485-1536 AKG London; p45 Portrait of Catherine Howard (c. 1520-d.1542) 5th Queen of Henry VIII from "Memoirs of the Court of Queen Elizabeth', published in 1825 (w/c and gouache on paper) by Sarah Countess of Essex (d. (1838) Private Collection/Bridgeman Art Library/The Stapleton Collection; p45 Portrait of Catherine Parr (1512-48) sixth wife of Henry VIII (1491-1547) (panel) by English School (16th Century) National Portrait Gallery, London UK, Roger-Viollet, Paris/Bridgeman Art Library; p45 Jane Seymour (1509-37) AKG London; p47 (a), (d) and (f) MC Archive, p47 (c) William McKeller/Alamy, (b) Jacqui Hurst/Corbis; e David Wall/Alamy; p50 Corbis; p63 top Ronald Grant Archive; p63 bottom The Broad Art Foundation © ADAGP Paris, and DACS London 2004; p68 Associated Press, AP; p69 All, Hart Mcleod; p72 D K Khattiya/Alamy; p80 Topham Picturepoint; p82 By permission of Margaret Johnson/Cambridge University Press; p89 Lina Ahnoff; pp95-96, Reeve Photography; p99 (Carol) BananaStock/Alamy, (Daniel) Jon Feingersh/Corbis, (Carmen) Steve Prezant/ Corbis, (Vince) Mark Anderson/Rubberball/Alamy, (electric guitar) Skye/Alamy, (drums) Alley Cat Productions/Brand X Pictures/Alamy, (saxophone) Curt Clayton/Alamy (cello) Richard Cummins/ Corbis, (guitar) Ingram Publishing/Alamy, (trumpet) Royalty-Free/Corbis.

Text acknowledgements

p18, based on Plane crashes into house ©Daily Mail 02/04/01; p37 left, The Confession ©Brian Patten; p37 right, I am Completely Different, translation ©James Kirkup, original ©Karoda Saburo; p54 Marathon marriage just the tip of the iceburg, based on Angel of the Bridge ©Daily Mail 23/04/01; p83 All I Want ©Margaret Johnson;p91, Not just a man's game, based on Something for the Ladies ©Stephanie Merritt, Observer Sports Monthly, April 2001;

Marshall Cavendish ELT
119 Wardour Street
London W1F 0UW

Designed by Hart McLeod, Cambridge
Editorial development by Ocelot Publishing, Oxford
Illustrations by Yane Christiansen, Rod Hunt, Jennifer Ward, Phil Healey, Clive Goodyear and Francis Fung

Contents

Unit 1   5
What are you like?

Unit 2   12
A narrow escape

Unit 3   19
What shoppers want

Unit 4   27
Away from it all

Unit 5   35
Home

Unit 6   42
Lives

Unit 7   50
Good intentions

Unit 8   58
You can't do that here!

Unit 9   65
Body talk

Unit 10   72
Technocrazy

Unit 11   79
Pictures and words

Unit 12   87
Not an easy game

Unit 13   95
More than music

Unit 14   103
Getting along

Audioscript   111

**Table of
phonemic symbols**   123

UNIT 1 What are you like?

Vocabulary: occupations and character description

1 Rearrange the letters to make the occupations.

a (d e g i n s   e e e g i n n r)

..... design engineer ....

b (a b o e f l l r t o)

....

c (a i j n o r s l t u)

....

d (a r c e h l o r s t   c c d n o u o r t)

....

e (a i m p r r y   a c e e h r t)

....

f (f g e h r f i r i t e)

....

g (o d e i l r s)

....

h (e n r s u)

....

i (s a e l n o p r   a a i n s s s t t)

....

j (e e f r s u   e c c l l o o r t)

....

2 Using some of the words in the box, or their opposites (for example *indecisive*), complete the following sentences. The first one is done for you.

> decisive ◆ enthusiastic ◆ friendly ◆ honest ◆
> hospitable ◆ kind ◆ loyal ◆ patient ◆ romantic ◆
> sensitive ◆ sincere ◆ sympathetic

a Steve can never make decisions. He is very
..... indecisive ....

b You can believe what they say. The staff seem
very ....

c You never feel welcome in Lisa's house. She's
very ....

d Your son is very .... He's always
telling lies.

e .... people are kind, listen to
your troubles, and try to help.

f Andrew gets very .... if he has to
wait too long for anything.

g In fairy stories stepmothers are often very
.... to their stepdaughters, though
no one really knows why.

h Don't expect Derek to cry when he sees moving
films. He's a very .... person!

i Anna's always keen on things – she always likes
to get involved. She's a very ....
person.

j It is easy to offend John because he's a very
.... man.

k Yumi will always defend you when other people
are attacking you. She's very ....

Reading

3 Read the story of Eugene Onegin and put the pictures (*a–f*) in the right order.

1 .... 2 .... 3 .... 4 .... 5 .... 6 ....

One of the greatest works of Russian literature is the poem *Eugene Onegin* by Aleksandr Pushkin (1799–1837). Ever since its publication in 1825 it has remained popular. It was made into an opera by the Russian composer Tchaikovsky and, a few years ago, into a film starring the British actor Ralph Ffienes.

The story of Eugene Onegin tells of Madam Larina, a widow, who lives in the country with her two daughters, Olga and Tatiana. Olga is more cheerful and outgoing than her younger sister who spends her time reading romantic novels. Olga is engaged to the young landowner, Lensky.

One day Lensky brings a friend from the city (St Petersburg) to visit Madam Larina and her daughters. He is Eugene Onegin, a man who has decided to be cynical, unemotional and bored by life. Tatiana doesn't realise this and falls passionately in love with him almost the moment she sees him. She writes a letter to tell him so, pouring out her adolescent heart, sure that he will answer her. But Onegin does not love Tatiana, of course. At least he does not love 'love', and so he tells her not to be so ridiculous. Tatiana is heartbroken.

A few days later Madam Larina throws a big party for Tatiana's birthday. People come from all the estates near hers, and there is much dancing and singing. Onegin is there too, but he is in a strange mood and, for his own amusement, he starts flirting with Olga. He jokes with her and dances with her, so that Lensky is first jealous and then absolutely furious. He challenges Onegin to a duel.

The next morning, early, while the mist still hangs over the lake near Madam Larina's house, the two men meet. They both know that fighting each other is stupid, but they can't stop what is about to happen. They take out their pistols. Onegin fires first and Lensky, his friend, falls to the ground. Onegin has killed him and so he has no choice but to leave – and quickly. He goes to live abroad, away from Russia.

Three years later he returns to St Petersburg. Enough time has passed, he thinks, for people to have forgotten about Lensky's death. On his first night back home he goes to a big ball. All of St Petersburg society is there.

Onegin sees a beautiful young girl dancing with her elderly husband, Prince Gremin. He can hardly take his eyes off her and realises, suddenly, that it is Tatiana, and realises, too, that he loves her – that he has always loved her. In an ironic twist of fate he now writes her his own letter pouring out his love for her. She agrees to meet him, and he begs her to leave her husband to be with him.

Tatiana is torn between her feelings for Onegin (who she still loves) and her duty to Prince Gremin (who is kind to her and to whom, after all, she is married). She is angry with Onegin. Why has it taken him so long to realise how he feels about her? If only, if only. She tells him he has come too late, that however much she wants to she cannot walk away from her marriage. This time it is Eugene Onegin who leaves the meeting with a broken heart, to walk the streets of St Petersburg in misery.

And in a final twist of fate in 1837 the writer of the poem, Pushkin, was himself killed in a duel just like Lensky, the character in the story.

4 Answer the following questions. The first one is done for you.

a Who challenges Onegin to a duel? ....*Lensky*....

b Who falls in love with Onegin? ....

c Who has a fiancée called Olga? ....

d Who has two daughters? ....

e Who kills Lensky? ....

f Who starred in a film of *Eugene Onegin*? ....

g Who married Tatiana? ....

h Who asks Tatiana to leave her husband? ....

i Who writes letters? ....

j Who wrote the opera *Eugene Onegin*? ....

k Who wrote the poem *Eugene Onegin*? ....

l Who died in 1837? ....

5 Look at the way the following words are used in the story of Eugene Onegin and then write them in the sentences. The first one is done for you.

a twist of fate ◦ cannot walk away from ◦ challenge someone to a duel ◦ fictional ◦ heartbroken ◦
in a strange mood ◦ landowner ◦ outgoing ◦ passionately ◦ pours out their heart ◦ ridiculous ◦ widow

a If someone is a ....*widow*...., it means her husband has died.

b If someone ...., it means they tell you honestly and passionately how they feel.

c If someone ...., it means they are asking someone to fight them, perhaps to the death.

d If someone .... something, it means they cannot abandon it.

e If someone is ...., it means they feel different from usual and other people notice this.

f If someone is .... in love, it means they are very, very much in love.

g If someone is ...., it means they talk a lot, are friendly and enjoy meeting people.

h If someone is ...., it means someone they love has left them or died and they are very sad.

i If someone is a ...., it means they have some land.

j If someone is a .... character, it means they do not really exist, but they are in a story, film or play.

k If something is ...., it means it is silly, not sensible.

l We call it .... when a strange, unexpected thing happens.

Grammar: present tenses

6 Jacky Beadle is talking on the telephone about the man she works for. Write the most appropriate form of the verbs (in brackets) in the gaps. The first one is done for you.

a Yes, Malcolm Clarke ....*is*.... a member of staff here. (be)

b I'm sorry, Mr Clarke isn't here. He .... a conference in Warsaw. (attend)

c He usually .... in his office from nine till three. (work)

d Yes, Mr Clarke .... to quite a lot of conferences. (go)

e At the conference in Warsaw, they.................... global warming. (discuss)

f Yes, Mr Clarke .... global warming is a problem. Why? Because it .... warmer all the time. (believe; get)

g He .... here for about six months of the year, and the rest of the time he .... around the world. (live; travel)

h He usually .... by plane. (go)

i He .... at the Meridien hotel in Warsaw. (stay)

j I don't know, but I hope that he .... a good time. (have)

k No, I'm sorry. I .... questions like that. We .... people's phone numbers or addresses. (not/answer; not/give)

7 Use the following prompts to make some of the caller's questions (from Exercise 6) about Mr Clarke. The first one is done for you.

a Malcolm Clarke - a member of staff there?

Is Malcolm Clarke a member of staff there?

b at work – when?

....

c discussing in Warsaw – what?

....

d Mr Clarke – believe – global warming is a problem?

....

e why – believe – he – global warming is a problem?

....

f Mr Clarke – travel a lot?

....

g he travel – how?

....

h staying in Warsaw – where?

....

i Mr Clarke – have a good time?

....

8 Jacky is having coffee with her sister Sarah. She is talking about her boss (Mr Clarke). Put the correct form of the verbs from the box in the gaps. The first one is done for you.

> not be ◆ not drive ◆ not enjoy ◆ feel ◆ get ◆ go ◆ grow ◆ have ◆ leave (x2) ◆ like (x3) ◆ live ◆ make ◆ realise ◆ seem ◆ speak ◆ take ◆ take part ◆ travel ◆ visit

He (a) ....*lives*.... in North London with his wife (a doctor), two children, a dog and a cat. He (b).................. a taxi to work every day because he (c) .... – he (d) .... it, you see.

He (e) .... a lot. He (f).................. all our overseas offices. At the moment he (g).................. in a conference in Warsaw. He (h) .... about pollution and the environment.

Everybody really (i) .... Malcolm, but he is a bit forgetful. He (j) .... his things on trains or in taxis. When he (k) .... that he's left some papers or his briefcase in some car or on some train, he (l) .... crazy and we (m) .... to start telephoning all over London – well all over the world, sometimes – to try and find his things. But he (n) .... stupid. He just (o) .... to be. Actually he's pretty clever.

The reason why everybody (p) .... Malcolm? Well, you see, the company (q) .... all the time. We're (r) .... big plans for the future, and everybody (s) .... very optimistic. We know that's because of Malcolm. He often (t) .... brilliant ideas and everybody (u) .... him a lot – I've said that already, haven't I!

That's why we're all a bit sad. He (v) .... the company in two weeks. He's going to travel the world and write a novel.

Functional language: meeting people

9 Put the words and punctuation in the correct order to make sentences. Write them in the correct place in the conversation.

a / coincidence / . / That's
teacher / be / you / a / ? /young / bit / Aren't / to / a
a / ask / Can/ ? / I / question / you
? / Do / enjoy / studying / you / zoology
him/ I / like / . / think / you'll
a / I'm / . / teacher
, / . / meet / nice / to / too / Yeah / you
someone / I'd / like / meet / . / to / There's / you

SUSAN: Come with me, Ruth. **(a)** ....

RUTH: Oh, that sounds interesting.

SUSAN: Yes, well **(b)** .... Mark, this is Ruth.

MARK: Nice to meet you Ruth

RUTH: **(c)** ....

MARK: What do you do?

RUTH: I'm a zoology student.

MARK: Oh really. **(d)** ....

RUTH: I don't really know. I've only just got here. My course hasn't started. But what about you? What do you do?

MARK: **(e)** ....

RUTH: Oh really. What do you teach?

MARK: Zoology.

RUTH: **(f)** ....

MARK: Yes, I suppose it is.

RUTH: **(g)** ....

MARK: Of course.

RUTH: **(h)** ....

MARK: Yes, I suppose I am. But like you, I've only just started.

Listening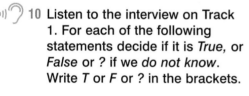

10 Listen to the interview on Track 1. For each of the following statements decide if it is *True,* or *False* or *?* if we *do not know.* Write *T* or *F* or *?* in the brackets.

Miss Franklin:
a ... gets the job.   [   ]
b ... likes hard work.   [   ]
c ... likes dancing in night   [   ]
   clubs.
d ... has a lot of hobbies.   [   ]
e ... has a boyfriend in the   [   ]
   company.
f ... thinks her boyfriend's   [   ]
   company will be friendly.

11 Can you remember the interviewers' questions? Use the words in brackets to write their questions. Then listen to Track 1 again, to see if you are right.

a (why/leave/last job?) ....

b (can/work on your own?) ....

c (what/not working?) ....

d (hobbies?) ....

e (why/want/this job?) ....

f (what/told you/our company?) ....

g (have/any questions for us?) ....

Would you give Miss Franklin the job? Why? Why not? Write your opinion.

12 Read the audioscript of Track 1 on page 111. Look up any words you do not know in your dictionary.

Pronunciation: intonation

13 Read the questions and listen to Track 2. Does the speaker's voice go *up* or *down* at the end of the question in each case? Circle the correct word.

a What do you think of Lisa?   up/down

b What do you do in advertising?   up/down

c Have you two met before?   up/down

d How long have you known Ruth?   up/down

e Can I ask you a question?   up/down

f Do you enjoy studying zoology?   up/down

g What time is your taxi coming?   up/down

Say the questions in the same way as the speakers on Track 2.

Writing: linking words

14 Join the following pairs of sentences/phrases with *although*, *because*, *despite*, or *in spite of*.

a Mary's friendliness! She can be very unkind. (in spite of)

In spite of Mary's friendliness, she can be very unkind.

b People think Annie is kind. She helps people all the time. (because) ....

c Sofia makes a lot of mistakes. She is not unintelligent. (although) ....

d Jill's keen on aeroplanes. She doesn't like flying. (although) ....

e Della's romanticism! She's never been in love. (despite) ....

f Carew's usual enthusiasm. She's feeling a bit low at the moment. (in spite of)...............

g I trust Lizzie. She's honest. (because)...............

h Laura often gets invited to parties. She's very interesting. (because) ....

15 Choose one of the people below or someone from a popular story in your culture. Imagine them as a school child. Write a report about them, using words from Exercise 2 and any others you think are appropriate. You can use the report on the witch as an example.

Cruella de Ville in 101 Dalmatians

FRANKENSTEIN'S MONSTER

Captain Hook in Peter P

The Wicked Witch in Sleeping Beauty

Name: The Wicked Witch

Principal's comments:

Although the witch is intelligent and works hard, she is unkind to her classmates, and she is often very unfriendly. She is not a very patient person and must try harder to be an enthusiastic member of the class.

Signed: Alfred P Bumble

REFLECTIONS

Thinking about learning and language: unit review

16 Complete the following table.

What I enjoyed most in Unit 1 (and why):	
Things I learnt that I did not know (or know how to do) before:	
Things I am going to do to help me remember what I have learnt in Unit 1:	
Things I found difficult in Unit 1 (and why):	
Questions I would like to ask my teacher about what we have done:	

Test your knowledge

17 Translate these sentences and questions into your own language.

a Although Peter is very loyal, he isn't very romantic.

....

b He doesn't work very hard. He just does the minimum.

....

c He's always been very keen on engineering.

....

d How are you getting on?

....

e There's someone I'd like you to meet.

....

f What are you working on at the moment?

....

g Would you keep an eye on things while I'm away?

....

h You have to be more assertive if you want to get on.

....

Did you have problems? If you did, go back to the relevant Activity in the Student's Book to check on meaning and use.

The phonemic alphabet

18 Consult the table of phonemic symbols on page 123 and then write these words in ordinary spelling.

a /əˈsɜːtɪv/ ....

b /ˈlɔɪjəl/ ....

c /ʌnˈkaɪnd/ ....

d /sɪnˈsɪə/ ....

e /ɪndəˈsaɪsɪv/ ....

f /kənˈsɪdərət/ ....

Check your answers by listening to Track 3.

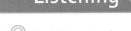

UNIT 2 | A narrow escape

Listening

1 Listen to the news report on Track 4. Are the following sentences *True* or *False*? Write *T* or *F* in the brackets.

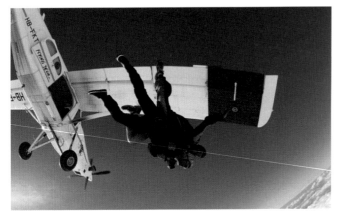

a Someone died.   [ ]
b A parachute failed to open properly.   [ ]
c The second parachute opened properly.   [ ]
d Two people broke bones.   [ ]
e The man has terrible injuries,
   the woman is less seriously injured.   [ ]
f It was the woman's first parachute jump.   [ ]
g The woman wants to do a parachute
   jump again.   [ ]

2 Listen to Track 4 again and answer the questions with the names from the box.

Beverly ◆ Dennis ◆ Jim ◆ Kevin ◆ Peter ◆ Sue

Who:

a ... parachuted together? ....

b ... is reporting from France? ....

c ... is in the studio in London? ....

d ... is in hospital? ....

e ... reported from the United Nations?

   ....

f ... was on honeymoon? ....

g ... thinks it was just pure luck? ....

h ... has a broken leg, a broken ankle and two

   broken feet? ....

i ... has just a broken leg? ....

j ... enjoys seeing the daylight and the birds?

   ....

3 Complete this audioscript with words and phrases from the box.

emergency chute ◆ faster and faster ◆
first parachute (x2) ◆ going to die ◆
hit the ground ◆ pure luck ◆
second emergency parachute ◆
solve the problem

REPORTER: The accident happened when the
(**a**) .... didn't open properly.
Mr McIlwee tried to (**b**) ...., but
when he couldn't, he tried to get rid of that
chute and use the (**c**) .... that
skydivers always carry with them. A few hours
ago I spoke to Beverly's father, Dennis
Murtaugh, who explains what happened next.
His words are spoken by an actor because the
line was not good when we talked.

DENNIS: Unfortunately, Kevin wasn't able to
jettison the (**d**) .... properly, so
the (**e**) .... wouldn't open and
they just fell (**f**) .... Kevin told
me that they thought that was it, they were
(**g**) ....

REPORTER: So how did they survive?

DENNIS: It was (**h**) .... I mean
they only had half a parachute to slow them
down. They (**i**) .... at an
absolutely fantastic speed. It could have killed
them.

Listen to Track 4 to check if you were correct.

Vocabulary: stronger adjectives

4 Find eight 'stronger' adjectives in the word puzzle.
One has been done for you.

f	u	r	i	o	u	s	a	b	c	d	f
a	p	o	n	m	l	k	j	i	h	g	r
n	q	r	s	t	u	v	w	x	y	z	e
t	e	r	r	i	b	l	e	b	c	d	e
a	f	g	h	i	b	j	k	l	m	n	z
s	p	q	r	s	t	o	u	v	w	x	i
t	e	r	r	i	f	y	i	n	g	a	n
i	b	n	c	d	h	e	f	l	g	h	g
c	d	e	o	t	j	k	l	m	i	n	o
p	q	r	l	r	s	t	u	v	w	n	x
y	z	i	a	b	m	c	d	e	f	g	g
h	f	i	j	k	l	o	m	n	o	p	q
r	s	t	u	v	w	x	u	y	z	a	b
m	l	k	j	i	h	g	f	s	e	d	c
n	o	p	q	r	s	t	u	v	w	x	y

5 Using the adjectives and adverbs from the boxes, complete these exchanges. The first one has been done for you.

Adverbs	Adjectives
absolutely	boiling ◆ enormous ◆ fantastic ◆
completely	filthy ◆ freezing ◆ furious ◆
really	terrible ◆ terrifying

a 'Look at my new picture.'
'Wow! It's ......*absolutely*......
.....*enormous!*..... ,

b 'What did your father say when you told him?'
'He was ....
.... ,

c 'Did you enjoy the meal he cooked for us?'
'No, it was ....
.... ,

d 'What do you think of the new CD?'
'It's ....
.... ,

e 'Why are you looking at me like that?'
'You're ....
.... ,

f 'Where are you going?'
'To have a swim. I'm
....
.... ,

g 'Did you enjoy the movie?'
'It was ....
.... ,

h 'Are you warm enough in your tent?'
'No, I'm ....
.... ,

6 Complete the conversation with one word for each gap.

BRIAN: Did you see *The Sixth Sense* on

(**a**) .... last night?

DAVE: No. But I (**b**) .... it when it first

came out some years (**c**) ....

BRIAN: Oh well, I'd never seen it (**d**) ....

so I was looking forward to it.

DAVE: What did you (**e**) .... of it?

BRIAN: It was absolutely terrifying.

DAVE: (**f**) .... you really think so?

BRIAN: Why? Don't you (**g**) .... with me?

DAVE: No, not really. I (**h**) .... it was

rather boring when I saw it, I remember.

BRIAN: (**i**) .... ? You can't be serious.

DAVE: Why not? I mean I (**j**) .... what

the ending was going to be (**k**) ....

the first five minutes.

BRIAN: Did you? I (**l**) .... I never

guessed.

DAVE: Oh well. But I (**m**) .... the little

boy was good.

BRIAN: Yes, I thought so (**n**) .... He

was completely believable.

FELICITY: Hi you (**o**) .... What are you

talking about?

BRIAN: That (**p**) .... , *The Sixth Sense*. It

was on the box (**q**) .... night.

FELICITY: Oh yes. I videoed it. I'm (**r**) ....

to watch it later. Will I enjoy it?

DAVE: (**s**) .... not. It's not a great

(**t**) .... , frankly.

BRIAN: Don't listen to him. It is a (**u**) ....

film. Really frightening.

DAVE: I don't (**v**) .... at all. I mean you

guess almost (**w**) .... that the

main character, the Bruce Willis character,

(**x**) .... a ...

BRIAN: Don't tell her the ending Dave, you

(**y**) .... ruin it for her. That's not

fair.

DAVE: You're (**z**) .... right. Sorry.

7 Complete the verb table. The first one is done for you.

infinitive	past form	past participle	infinitive	past form	past participle
a. arrive	*arrived*	*arrived*	j. see		
b. be			k. meet		
c. bring			l. know		
d. buy			m. ring		
e. do			n. send		
f. eat			o. start		
g. feel			p. drink		
h. get			q. tell		
i. have					

8 Make questions using the prompts in brackets and the question word in blue. The first one is done for you.

a (Tim asked you something then)

what _What did Tim ask you then?_

b (he had come over to speak to you)

why ....

c (he was talking about something)

what ....

d (Diana got there)

when ....

e (you first saw Tim)

when ....

f (you said something)

what ....

g (you said that)

why ....

h (you thought something about that)

what ....

i (you were waiting for someone)

who ....

9 Now here are the answers to the questions in Exercise 8. Choose the question that goes with each answer and write it in the correct space. The first one is done for you.

a _Question e_ ....

– My second week in college. I was waiting for someone in the canteen when he came in.

b ....

– Diana, a friend of mine.

c ....

– About ten minutes later. But Tim was talking to me when she came in.

d ....

– I can't remember what he was talking about.

e ....

– Because he said he thought I looked 'interesting'. That's why.

f ....

– Not much!

g ....

– He asked me to go to the cinema with him.

h ....

– I told him no.

i ....

– Because I'd already seen the film

10 Read the newspaper article below and then complete the table.

	Name(s)	Occupation(s)
People who live in the house:		
Pilot:		

My amazing escape

(from *The Daily Mail*)

When Helen Monahan got a phone call asking her to pick up a friend's children from school while collecting her own, she grabbed her coat and headed down the road.

It meant leaving home five minutes earlier than she had intended – but it could also have saved her life.

Minutes after she shut the door, a light aircraft crashed onto her empty house.

'I am trying not to think what would have happened if I had left home at the normal time,' said Mrs Monahan.

Pilot Donald Campbell also had reason to be thankful. The 52-year-old neurosurgeon walked away from the wreckage with only minor injuries to his face and head.

He had been steering the four-seater Piper Seneca towards Shoreham Airport in West Sussex when the twin engines cut out.

It plunged and clipped a railway bridge, before ploughing through the roof of the £150,000 three-bedroom house in the town of Shoreham-by-Sea.

It toppled into the back garden, which was strewn with children's toys.

Mrs Monahan, 36, said: 'It looks like something out of a film set. The tail of the plane was up in the air and the nose was in the fish pond.' Her husband Marcus, a 33-year-old boiler engineer, was at work at the time of the crash, and their children – Harley, six, and five-year-old Norton – were in school.

Mr Campbell, who flies all over the country to treat the patients of his private practice, said: 'I was coming into the airport and both engines cut out. It began to yaw quite sharply to one side.

'I couldn't land on the railway line because of the electric cable and I saw a gap by the houses and aimed next to them.

'I remember a bang. The port wing tip must have hit the roof. It was a bit rough.'

Safety officials were last night examining the plane to try to discover what went wrong.

11 Is each of the following statements *True* or *False*? Write *T* or *F* in the brackets.

a Mrs Monahan collected two children from school on the day of the crash. [ ]
b Nobody was seriously hurt in the crash. [ ]
c The pilot knows why the engines stopped suddenly. [ ]
d The pilot tried to land on the railway line. [ ]
e The pilot flies a lot. [ ]
f There were children's toys in the garden before the aeroplane landed there. [ ]
g The first thing that the plane hit was the roof. [ ]

12 Look at the way the verbs in the box are used in the newspaper report and then write each one next to the correct dictionary definition below. The first one is done for you.

clip ◆ cut out ◆ grab ◆ pick up ◆ plough through
plunge ◆ steer ◆ treat ◆ yaw

a to collect someone who is waiting for you:
....*pick up*....

b to control the direction of a vehicle or aircraft:
....

c to fall or move down very quickly and with force:
....

d to get something quickly because you do not have much time: ....

e to give medical care to someone:
....

f to hit something quickly and lightly:
....

g to hit something with great force and then continue moving: ....

h to move away from its proper course:
....

i to suddenly stop working: ....

13 Look at this diagram of a Piper Seneca aeroplane. Label it with words from the text.

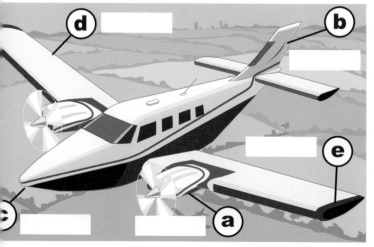

Writing: headlines

14 Match the columns to make newspaper headlines.

Adventure tourist says	see 26-goal defeat
Heroic stewardess	stranded fisherman
Horrified football fans	by escaped lion
Schoolboy attacked	in desert ordeal
Sharp-eyed sailor finds	saves trapped pilot
Travellers rescued	'Never again!'

a ....
b ....
c ....
d ....
e ....
f ....

15 Choose one of the headlines above and write the story about it for a local newspaper. Your article should be no more than three short paragraphs long.

Pronunciation: stress

16 Circle the stressed syllables in the adjectives and their *intensifiers* (words that make them stronger or weaker). Put a line under the strongest syllable. The first one is done for you.

a He's rather interesting.
b I was pretty scared.
c It was absolutely amazing.
d It was absolutely hilarious.
e She was rather angry.
f They're really good.
g Your room's absolutely filthy!

Listen to Track 5 and repeat the sentences.

REFLECTIONS

Thinking about learning and language: vocabulary

17 Complete the following sentences.

a When I come across a word I do not know, I ....
....
....

b The best way of finding out the meaning of a new word (for me)
is ....
....

c When I write down a new word in my notebook so that I can
remember it, I ....
....

18 Can you think of other ways of dealing with new vocabulary (apart
from the ways you described in Exercise 17)? Think of other
possibilities and complete the table with them.

a When I come across a new word:	
b How to find the meaning of a new word:	
c Ways of writing new words in my notebook:	

Test your knowledge

19 Which of the following sentences are written in correct English?
Put a tick (✓) or a cross (✗) in the brackets.

a After the fall, Mary lost conscience and didn't wake up for
some time. [   ]
b I met her at ten o'clock and we had gone to have coffee. [   ]
c I am sure I give him my telephone number yesterday. [   ]
d The film was absolutely amazing. [   ]
e When he opened his birthday present, he couldn't believe
his eye. [   ]
f When I arrived at the house, I was realising that I was late. [   ]
g When I got to work late, my boss was very furious. [   ]
h When I tried to pay the bill, I realised that I had left my
money at home. [   ]
i When I woke up last night, I couldn't get back to sleep. [   ]
j You think that the film was good, but I am not agree
with you. [   ]

Rewrite the items which you marked with a cross, to make correct
sentences.

The phonemic alphabet

20 Consult the table of phonemic
symbols on page 123 and then
write these words and phrases
in ordinary spelling.

a /əmˈeɪzɪŋ/ ....

b /ˈkɒnʃəs/ ....
....

c /hɪˈleərɪəs/ ....

d /prɪtɪjəmˈeɪzɪŋ/ ....
....

e /rɪˈmembəd/ ....
....

f /ʃɔː/ ....
....

g /ʌŋˈkɒnʃəs/ ....
....

◁)) Check your answers by listening
to Track 6.

UNIT 3 What shoppers want

Vocabulary: shopping and supermarkets

1 Write the number from the picture for the items below.

air extractor   [ ] aisle   [ ]
counter   [ ] customer   [ ]
entrance   [ ] exit   [ ]
security camera [ ] sell-by date   [ ]
shopping list   [ ] shelf   [ ]
shopping bag   [ ] shopping trolley [ ]
vacuum-packed   [ ]

2 Complete the questionnaire with *shopping* and one of the words or phrases from the blue box.
Circle the answer you would give.
Follow the first example.

do the ◆ expedition ◆ go ◆
Internet ◆ last-minute ◆
late-night ◆ trolley ◆ window-

SHOPPING QUESTIONNAIRE

a Do you ever go on a major ..shopping..expedition.. which lasts the whole day?	always / usually / often / sometimes / never
b Do you ever forget things and have to rush and do ....?	always / usually / often / sometimes / never
c Is it possible to do .... where you live or do all the shops close early?	always / usually / often / sometimes / never
d Do you ever spend time .... without actually buying anything?	always / usually / often / sometimes / never
e Do you ever .... at the end of a long day at work?	always / usually / often / sometimes / never
f Do you use a .... when you go to the supermarket?	always / usually / often / sometimes / never
g Do you ever .... for everyone in your house?	always / usually / often / sometimes / never
h Do you ever use your computer to do ....?	always / usually / often / sometimes / never

3   Read this page from a website and then circle the best answers on the next page.

printer version | email this article | send feedback

internet.com

SUBSCRIBE

Email Marketing

Technology

Advertising

Customer Care

Contact Us

Archives

Email Marketing

The Leading Edge

Brand Marketing

Media Buying

Site Design

Writing Online

Ecommerce Marketing

What Do Online Shoppers Want?

› › › The Leading Edge

When real life collides with Net life, it can really put things into perspective.

In Baltimore, Maryland we have just got a new shopping mall, and it's huge! The $250 million Arundel Mills Mall is one of the biggest shopping complexes in the United States. It has a movie theatre with more than twenty screens, there are enormous entertainment areas – and more than 7,000 parking spaces.

During its opening weekend two weeks ago, the place was a madhouse, with huge traffic queues on the exit ramps leading to the mall that extended for miles as tens of thousands of cars tried to get into too few parking spaces. Police patrolled the highways to keep shoppers from parking up to ten miles away on the side of the road and walking to the mall.

And since that opening weekend people haven't just come to look. They're buying, too. They've already spent several million dollars, and this is just the beginning of the Christmas shopping season. And every day there are stories about it on the TV or in the local papers. It's a huge success.

Shopping on the Internet isn't a success like that. True it's growing, but very slowly. People still seem to prefer the real offline experience to buying things from the comfort of their own home.

But why? Why do so many people spend so much money offline while the online sector is still creeping along? When I drove by the lines of cars going to my friendly neighborhood megamall, I thought long and hard about this question. Those people sitting in their cars (some for more than an hour!) clearly weren't there for convenience. They weren't there because they expected exceptional customer service. Sure, many of them were there because this monster was new and different and something to gawk at, but many of them were spending money.

As I drove by, all I kept asking myself was "When was the last time anybody got this excited about a new e-commerce site? Is shopping online somehow fundamentally different than shopping offline?"

I've begun to think it is, especially now that studies are showing us how and why people use (and don't use) the Internet to shop. For example one recent report shows that people only start buying on the web when they've been Internet users for some time. So people in Sweden (who've had the Internet for quite a few years) buy more than people from France (who haven't had the Internet for as long). You have to feel comfortable before you shop online!

The most successful shopping sites on the Internet are small – the ones that only offer one thing. They're quick, easy to use, don't ask for too much personal information (something that stops many people from shopping on the Internet), and don't go wrong in the middle of a shopping session. I think I now understand what it's all about. As my recent megamall experience proved to me, people in the real world are a lot more willing to put up with a lot of hassles in order to be immersed in an experience that may have shopping at its core, but also includes social and entertainment aspects. Online, it's a different story. In the end, sites that concentrate on the basics of customer focus, relevance, support, service, fulfilment, and function are the ones that are going to win ... not the ones that try to fight the megamalls.

a The Arundel Mills Mall:

1 ... is a new American online Internet site.

2 ... is a new shopping centre in the United States.

3 ... is a new hospital for people with mental problems.

b The article says that Internet shopping sites are most successful when:

1 ... they try to be like the kind of shopping people do in huge megamall shopping centres.

2 ... the customers are new Internet users.

3 ... they are small and efficient and don't try to be like megamalls.

c People who go to the megamall:

1 ... go because it is convenient and the staff are extremely efficient.

2 ... go because police patrol the highways.

3 ... go for an 'experience' which includes shopping and entertainment.

d People from Sweden buy more on the Internet than people from France because:

1 ... the Internet has been in Sweden longer than it has been in France.

2 ... the Internet hasn't been in Sweden as long as it has been in France.

3 ... Swedish Internet sites are very small.

4 Match the words and phrases from the text (in the box) with their definitions. The first one is done for you.

a a 'place' you visit when you use your computer to connect to the Internet: ...site...

b a line of people or things waiting to go somewhere: ....

c a period of the year when a particular thing happens:

....

d a place where there is a lot of confusing noise and activity:

....

e short roads that are used to drive off larger main roads:

....

f connected to an Internet site: ....

g something that is annoying because it is difficult or chaotic:

....

h to bump into: ....

i to walk around to make sure things are all right in an area or building: ....

j to move somewhere very slowly: ....

k something which helps you to understand how important or unimportant something is: ....

l when something is easy to use and useful for what you need:

....

m when you go shopping in the real world: ....

n working well – without wasting time or effort: ....

collide

convenience

creep along

efficient

exit ramps

hassle

madhouse

online

patrol

put things into perspective

queue

season

shopping offline

site

5 Complete the tables below with notes about (*a*) the megamall, and (*b*) online shopping sites, from pages 20 and 21.

a The megamall

1 Name of the mall:	
2 Cost:	
3 Location:	
4 Number of parking spaces:	
5 What's in it:	
6 Longest queues on the opening weekend:	

b Online shopping sites

1 People most likely to shop online:	
2 Qualities of good online sites:	
3 What online sites need if they are going to win:	

Grammar: quantifiers

6 Look at each sentence – is it saying something happy or sad? Draw a smiley face (☺) or a sad face (☹) for each sentence. The first one is done for you.

a A few people really like my new paintings. ☺

b Every time I talk to her she smiles. ◯

c Few people came to my party. ◯

d I have very little chance of passing this exam. ◯

e I'm not having much fun right now. ◯

f A lot of people really like my pictures. ◯

g My friend Elaine had little opportunity to visit me. ◯

h There are a lot of people in here. They've all come to see my paintings. ◯

i There are so many questions in the exam. I'm certain to get some of them right. ◯

j Very few people like my new paintings. ◯

7 Correct the mistakes in the following sentences. The first one is done for you.

a We don't get much shoppers here any more.

We don't get many shoppers here any more.

b People spend very few money in this shop.

....

c This will only take little time.

....

d There aren't any sugar in this tin.

....

e Every people likes coffee.

....

f I always drink coffee after all meal.

....

g I only take a few milk in my coffee.

....

h I'll come round in a little minutes.

....

i Finding a good bargain in the shops gives me many satisfaction.

....

8 Complete the sentences with one word for each gap. Use each of the quantifiers in the box once.

a bit of ◆ a few ◆ a lot of ◆ any ◆ every ◆ few ◆ many ◆ several ◆ some ◆ very little

a .... shop on this street has closed since they built that new supermarket.

b .... people actually enjoy buying clothes; most people don't really like doing it at all.

c I bought .... things on my last shopping expedition, but not as much as I had hoped.

d I can't see .... offers that interest me in today's sales. There's absolutely nothing here that I want to buy.

e I need .... help. This shopping is too heavy for one person to carry.

f I need .... encouragement to go window-shopping. It's my favourite hobby.

g People come here all the time because they like the atmosphere – and I mean .... people. The place is usually very crowded.

h .... people – not a lot, but more than just a few – complained about the noise in the shop today.

i .... people found it difficult to get to the supermarket today because the roads were so crowded. The supermarket wasn't nearly as crowded as usual.

j There's .... a queue at that counter, but it shouldn't take too long.

Functional language: going shopping

9 Put the following lines in the correct place in the coversation.

1 Umm, actually, perhaps you can help me. I'm looking for a fleece.
2 No thanks, I'm just looking around.
3 Oh right. Thanks.
4 Oh, umm, excuse me, just before I go and look at the fleeces, do you have any of those Arguski belts – you know the brown and red ones?
5 Thanks.
6 Thanks. Good idea. I'll go there now.
7 That's a pity. Do you know where I could buy one of those belts?
8 They'll sell them in the department store opposite, won't they?

A: Can I help you?

B: **(a)** ....

A: OK. Let me know if I can help you with anything.

B: **(b)** ....

A: No problem.

B: **(c)** ....

A: Oh right. The fleeces are over there by the jeans.

B: **(d)** ....

A: You're welcome.

B: **(e)** ....

A: No, I'm sorry. We don't sell Arguski designs.

B: **(f)** ....

A: You could try the department store opposite. They might be able to help.

B: **(g)** ....

A: But what about the fleeces?

B: **(h)** ....

A: Yes. I suppose they will.

Look at the picture. What is the assistant's mistake?

....

....

🔊 **10** Listen to the interview on Track 7. As you listen to the man's answers, cross out any information that is incorrect in the questionnaire below, and write in the correct answer. The first one is done for you.

QUESTIONNAIRE FORM Q3657

(For each question, tick the appropriate box.)

Q1 How often do you go shopping?

once a week [✓]
twice a week [✓]
three times a week [ ]
more than three times [ ]

Q2 How many items do you buy when you go shopping?

1 item [✓]
2 items [ ]
3–5 items [ ]
6–10 items [ ]
10+ items [ ]

Q3 How much time do you spend when you go shopping?

0–59 minutes [✓]
1–2 hours [ ]
more than 2 hours [ ]

Q4 What do you buy most often?

trousers [ ]
shirts [✓]
underwear [ ]
T-shirts [ ]
jackets [ ]
sweaters [ ]

Q5 Favourite colour (state item of clothing)?

....

....

....

11 Rearrange the words in brackets to make sentences from the interview. Then listen to Track 7 again. Which reply (from the box below) follows each sentence? The first one is done for you.

a (a/a/bit/hurry/of/I'm/./in)

   I'm in a bit of a hurry. .... [7]

b (automatically/be/draw/entered/in our prize/ ./You'll)

   .... [ ]

c (are/chances/of/?/my/What/winning)

   .... [ ]

d (I/know/./wouldn't)

   .... [ ]

e (a/get/let's/move on/./But)

   .... [ ]

f (have/I/if/./only/to/But)

   .... [ ]

g (do/for fun/I/It's/not/./something)

   .... [ ]

h (be/./Don't/know/never/./You/pessimistic/so)

   .... [ ]

---

1 Oh yes I do. I never win anything!
2 Look this is really ...
3 OK, the fourth question ...
4 Right, well the first question is ....
5 Sorry?
6 The same as anybody else's, I suppose.
7 It'll only take a second.
8 Yes ... and how many items do you usually buy ... ?

GRAND HOLIDAY PRIZE DRAW

HOLIDAY FOR TWO IN JAMAICA

Writing: paragraph construction

12 Read the paragraph. Write the sentence number in the brackets for each of the following.

a Conclusion   [   ]
b Example/explanation   [   ]
c Exception/question   [   ]
d Introduction   [   ]

[1] All over the world huge shopping complexes are replacing town centres as the places where people go to buy things and to enjoy themselves. [2] The biggest is 'The Mall' in Minneapolis, USA, which has shops, restaurants, cinemas, and play areas for children, and one of the newest is 'CentrO' near Düsseldorf in Germany. [3] The only problem, according to some commentators, is that these huge centres create more traffic and are helping to destroy the heart of most towns. [4] However, as long as people want them, new shopping malls will continue to be built.

Write a similar 4-sentence paragraph about *Why I like/don't like shopping*.

Pronunciation: sounds

13 Listen to the pairs of sentences on Track 8. Are they the *Same* or *Different*? Write *S* or *D* in the brackets.

a [   ]

b [   ]

c [   ]

d [   ]

e [   ]

f [   ]

Listen to Track 8 again and repeat the sentences.

REFLECTIONS

Thinking about learning and language: reading

14 Answer the questions about how you read in your own language.

a Do you read each word separately, or do you read chunks of words (e.g. four at a time)?

....

.... [   ]

b Do your eyes move slowly from left to right on each line or do they move rapidly all over the page from one place to another?

....

.... [   ]

c Are you a slow reader or a fast reader?

....

.... [   ]

d Do you use a dictionary if you come across a word you do not know the meaning of?

....

.... [   ]

e Do you say the words either aloud or 'in your head' as you read them?

....

.... [   ]

Do you read in English in the same way? Now write *S* (*Same*) or *D* (*Different*) in the brackets for each answer you gave.

15 Look at these three different ways of reading.

Skimming: reading a complete text very quickly to get its general meaning
Scanning: looking at a text quickly just to find a specific piece of information
Reading for detail: reading a text carefully to understand everything it says

Write five different things you can read (e.g. a menu, a newspaper article, an instruction manual) and say which way of reading you would choose for each.

Things you can read:	Ways of reading of reading them:
a	....
b	....
c	....
d	....
e	....

Test your knowledge

16 Translate the following sentences and questions.

a   She was just window-shopping when I saw her.

   ....

b   Silence makes shoppers feel uncomfortable.

   ....

c   There isn't much choice in this supermarket.

   ....

d   I need very little money to live on.

   ....

e   Will you complete this questionnaire? It only takes a few minutes.

   ....

f   I'm just looking around.

   ....

g   You could try the shop on the corner.

   ....

h   Let me know if I can help you with anything.

   ....

Did you have problems? If you did, go back to the relevant activity in the Student's Book to check on meaning and use.

The phonemic alphabet

17 Consult the table of phonemic symbols on page 123 and then write these words and phrases in ordinary spelling.

a /fliːs/..

   ....

b /ekspəd'ɪʃən/..

   ....

c /'sɪərɪjəs/..

   ....

d /suːpəmaːkɪt/..

   ....

e /'enɪθɪŋ/..

   ....

f /'sevrəl/..

   ....

g /'vækjuːmpækt/..

   ....

Check your answers by listening to Track 9.

Listening

1 When you are travelling, when and where do you hear public announcements? What do they usually say?

2 When would you hear these announcements? Look at the pictures (a–g) and listen to the announcements on Track 10. Write the number of the announcement (1–7) above the appropriate picture.

a ....

b ....

M	TIME	DESTINATIO
2	6:40	BIRMINGHAM
1	6:52	KING'S LYNN
3	6:55	MANCHESTE
1	6:59	LIVERPOOL
4	7:00	LONDON KI

c ....

d ....

FG0902	GATE CLOSED
BA2409	NOW BOARDING
BA2018	WAIT IN LOUNGE
VA0034	WAIT IN LOUNGE
TV0102	WAIT IN LOUNGE
BA0208	DELAYED
KL0123	WAIT IN LOUNGE
DA134	WAIT IN LOUNGE

e ....

MANCHESTER AIR

f ....

GATE 24

g ....

3 Complete these expressions from the announcements with the words or phrases from the box. Match them with the pictures. The first one is done for you.

> announcement ◆ board ◆ delay ◆ fasten ◆ fastened ◆ last call ◆ late ◆ place ◆ position ◆ proceed ◆ regret ◆ return ◆ running ◆ shouldn't ◆ sorry ◆ switched off

a This is the __last call__ for flight 2409. [d]

b Please .... to gate number 35. [ ]

c Here is a platform .... [ ]

d We are ready to .... the aircraft. [ ]

e We .... to announce the .... of the 12.35. [ ]

f The train is .... approximately 15 minutes .... [ ]

g .... for the delay. [ ]

h We .... be here for too long. [ ]

i Will all passengers please .... to your seats. [ ]

j .... your seatbelts. [ ]

k .... your seats in the upright .... [ ]

l Please keep your seatbelts .... until the captain has .... the seatbelt sign. [ ]

Listen to Track 10 again to check your answers.

4 Complete the sentences with one word for each gap.

   a A holiday on a large ship is called a ....

   b I think activity holidays are really ....
      They're certainly not boring.

   c If you want to see things from many years ago

      you can visit a ....

   d People who spend too much time ....
      often get burnt.

   e People who go on holiday to see different

      places are called ....

   f Rooms that are .... - ....
      are always cooler than those that are not.

   g When you go on a holiday in which everything
      has been arranged for you, this is called a

      ....

5 Take the first letter of each answer from Exercise 4. Rearrange the letters to find where Henry is staying.

'We always stay on a _ _ _ _ _ _ e.'

6 Put the letters in order to make holiday and tourism words.

   a (a a b d o r)........................

   b (a a b c c g i k k n p)........................

   c (c e i n o r s u x)........................

   d (a e g l l r y)........................

   e (a a d e h i k l m o r y)........................

   f (e o r r s t)........................

   g (e e g g h i i n s s t)........................

   h (a a c i n o t v)........................

7 Read the text on page 29. Are the following sentences *True* (*T*) or *False* (*F*)?

   a The writer was woken up by gun shots. [   ]

   b The writer loved Mexico City. [   ]

   c Some people in Mexico City advised the
      writer to travel to Oaxaca. [   ]

   d The writer travelled by train. [   ]

   e The writer stayed in a luxury hotel. [   ]

   f The shower didn't work. [   ]

   g The writer had breakfast in the square. [   ]

   h The writer ordered 'huevos rancheross',
      orange juice and coffee. [   ]

   i It was probably going to be a sunny day. [   ]

   j The unfriendly man was the woman's
      boyfriend. [   ]

The following extract is taken from the novel *The Backpacker Journals* by Philip Douglas.
It is a thriller about the adventures of a traveller in Mexico.

I was woken by a noise like gun shots. I sat up in bed, half asleep and frightened. But it was only the roar of a passing truck, the noise of its engine filling the tiny side street.

I tried to remember where I was. I had arrived in Mexico City two days before on a cheap flight from New York. Mexico City is the biggest city in the world, and has more cars and noise than anywhere I had ever been. I soon realised that I would have to get away.

I met up with some other backpackers in the 'Zona Rosa' (the Pink Zone) as they shopped for souvenirs. They had just come back from the south and the place they liked best was a much smaller city called Oaxaca (pronounced 'Waharka' they said). It sounded fantastic. They told me about the pyramids at Monte Alban and the ruins at Mitla. There was even, they said, a place called El Tulle which had the biggest tree in, well, that part of Mexico, anyway.

That was enough for me. I went straight to the big 'TAPO' terminal and got the first long-distance bus I could find. The trouble was that it didn't arrive until late at night after a seven-hour trip. I ended up in the cheapest hotel I could find. Even for a backpacker like me, it was basic.

The noise of the truck disappeared and now all I could hear was the old electric fan by my bedside. I looked at my watch. It was a quarter to seven in the morning. Sleep was impossible. I was very tired, but wide awake – something that often happens to me when I travel.

I got out of bed and had a shower – the shower worked, and the water was hot. I put on some clean clothes and went out towards the main square which my friends from Mexico City had told me I should see.

Even at this early hour of the morning it was beginning to get warm. There was a café on the north side of the square. It was open. In front of me I could see a little park and a bandstand. A group of women walked past carrying baskets on their heads. There was a group of tourists about my age sitting at a table to my right. They were eating breakfast. It looked incredible and it smelt lovely.

The woman noticed me staring. She pointed at her plate.

'Delicious!' she laughed.

'What are they?' I couldn't help asking.

'"Huevos rancheros" – fried eggs in Mexican sauce.'

'They smell fantastic.'

'Taste fantastic too. You from Britain?'

'No. Australian. You?'

'American. From Arizona. This your first time here?'

'Yep. You?'

'Yes. Three days. I ...' but she stopped talking when one of the men at the table – her boyfriend I thought (wrongly, as it turned out later) - gave her an angry look.

A waiter came over to my table. He looked as if he hadn't slept much either.

It took a bit of time, but I ordered coffee, orange juice and some of the Mexican eggs the girl had told me about.

I looked back at the other table. The 'boyfriend' was staring at me and he didn't look friendly. I turned away.

8 Look at the way the words and phrases in the box are used in the text on page 29, and then write them in the correct gaps. The first one is done for you.

> bandstand • basic • get away • roar • ruins •
> souvenirs • staring • terminal • turned out •
> wide awake

a A ....*roar*.... is a loud noise, like the noise of an angry lion.

b When you .... from somewhere, you leave it, you escape from it.

c Tourists often buy .... , small presents to remind them of places and experiences.

d Parts of damaged buildings that have survived are called ....

e Another word for a large bus station is a bus ....

f Something that is very simple and not at all luxurious is often called ....

g If you are completely awake you are ....

h The place in a park or square where musicians play (with a roof, but no sides) is called a ....

i If something happened that you did not expect, you can say it .... differently.

j If someone is looking at you for some time, they are .... at you.

9 Copy and complete the table with the information required.

a the first sound in the morning:
b the noise next to the writer's bed:
c something at Monte Alban:
d something at Mitla:
e something at El Tulle:
f Write the rest of the conversation between the woman and the writer in complete sentences. (The first line is done for you.)   Woman: They're delicious!

Grammar: comparative and superlative adjectives (and adverbs)

10 Complete this table. The first word is done for you.

Word	Comparative form	Superlative form
a. cold	colder	coldest
b. angry		
c. honest		
d. pale		
e. good		
f. emotional		
g. kind		
h. sad		
i. blue		
j. fast		
k. slowly		
l. well		
m. kindly		
n. badly		
o. often		
p. much		
q. early		
r. frequently		

11 Look at the pictures and write a sentence comparing the things or people in the pictures.

a The white shoes are
....

b The short girl can run
....

John (20) Mike (15) Harry (9)

c John is ....

....

d The girl in the T-shirt must be

....

e The house on the left is

....

f The road on the right looks

....

12 Add one phrase from each of the two columns to make a sentence. You can only use each phrase once.

as keen on holidays as	a bit wiser.
it's hotter in December	better.
and more crowded	cities in the world.
more fun than	cruises.
more expensive	every year.
one of the most famous	her sister.
tall as	his sister.
the	I've ever had.
was the best one	than going by train.
we get	than in July.

a Brian isn't as ....

b Camping holidays are ....

c Flying is ....

d Heat? The hotter ....

e In Australia ....

f Last year's holiday ....

g Paris is ....

h She's not ....

i The roads are getting more ....

j Every year ....

13 Complete these sentences with one word for each gap.

a .... San Fransisco .... a visit?

b Can you .... a good place .... a holiday?

c Have you .... going to this five-star hotel in the mountains?

d What .... camping?

e I'd prefer something .... cheaper.

f .... Rio de Janeiro worth .... ?

g Well, what .... of holiday do you want?

h That .... like a .... idea.

i That's exactly what I .... for.

j Well, it's not my idea .... fun.

k That's not .... what we .... thinking of.

l Why don't you .... it?

14 Choose eight of the utterances from Exercise 13 to complete this conversation.

LUCY: (**a**) ....?

KIM: (**b**) ....

LUCY: Well we're looking for a bit of comfort, somewhere away from the city.

KIM: OK. (**c**) ....?

JIM: Isn't that rather expensive?

KIM: Well yes, but the mountain air is great and the views are fantastic.

JIM: I think we'd prefer something a bit more, well ....

LUCY: He means cheaper.

JIM: Yes, that's it. Cheaper.

KIM: (**d**) ....?

JIM: Camping? What, you mean in a tent?

KIM: Yes. There's a really good campsite in the same area.

JIM: No. (**e**) ....

LUCY: Oh come on, Jim, it might be fun.

JIM: (**f**) ....

KIM: Look, if it was me I'd always prefer to stay in a hotel or a hostel or something, but lots of people go camping and really love it. (**g**) ....?

LUCY: You know what? (**h**) ....

JIM: Does it?

LUCY: Sure it does. Tell us more about this mountain campsite.

KIM: OK. Well it's a five-hour bus journey from the city ...

15 Number the paragraphs from 1 – 7 to put them in the right order to make a composition about Christmas Day. The first one is done for you.

CHRISTMAS DAY

For Sarah Merrington, Christmas Day is the biggest family celebration of the year. Here she explains what happens every December 25th.

[ ] After breakfast we gather round the Christmas tree and open presents we have bought each other. And then, with some complaining, we get ourselves ready and set off for my grandmother's house.

[ ] Driving is OK on Christmas Day. There are no lorries on the road and fewer cars than usual, so we get to our destination in only about an hour and a half. By this stage, it's usually about half past twelve.

[ ] Every year we say we're going to do something different, but every year we do exactly the same!

[ ] Gradually everyone arrives – my uncles and aunts and cousins – and then we have something to drink and open some more presents. And then it's time for a huge lunch, with a large Christmas turkey and Christmas pudding. It's exactly the same every year.

[1] In my family the biggest family celebration of the year is Christmas Day, the 25th of December. Every year, even now we're grown up, we get up and find stockings full of small presents outside our bedroom doors. When we were little we used to believe that Father Christmas put them there, but we've known it was our parents for years!

16 Who or what are the following?

a .... b .... c .... d .... e ....

17 Think of the main family celebration of the year – or some other annual event that is always the same. Make notes about the information you will include when you write about it.

Based on your notes, now write a composition about the most important annual celebration in your family or your country.

[ ] The next morning, Boxing Day, we set off for my uncle's house – that's my father's brother – and open more presents and have another huge meal. And then, finally, later that afternoon, we set off home.

[ ] The rest of the day usually passes quietly because everyone has eaten too much, so we just sit around and chat or watch television.

Pronunciation: similar sounds

18 Listen to Track 11. Circle the word you hear.

a big pig
b hot hat
c cheap sheep
d nice noise
e good wood

f fat foot
g better wetter
h plane plan
i cruise choose
j sight seat

Listen to Track 11 again and repeat the words.

REFLECTIONS

Thinking about learning and language: listening

19 How much do you listen to the following? Circle the appropriate answer in each case.

English-speaking radio	all the time | often | sometimes | occasionally | never
English-speaking TV channels	all the time | often | sometimes | occasionally | never
English-speaking films (with or without subtitles)	all the time | often | sometimes | occasionally | never
English-language rock & pop CDs, mini-disks etc.	all the time | often | sometimes | occasionally | never
English-language Internet sites with audio	all the time | often | sometimes | occasionally | never
English-language speakers face-to-face	all the time | often | sometimes | occasionally | never
English-language speakers on the telephone	all the time | often | sometimes | occasionally | never
English-language announcements in stations/airports	all the time | often | sometimes | occasionally | never
Tapes made for English-language students	all the time | often | sometimes | occasionally | never
Videos/DVDs made especially for English-language students	all the time | often | sometimes | occasionally | never
Something else (describe it here):	all the time | often | sometimes | occasionally | never

20 Complete the following sentences about you and listening.

a I find listening in English easy/difficult because ....

....

b Listening to a tape is easier/more difficult than listening to a speaker you can see because ....

....

c When I listen to people speaking English I try/don't try to understand every word because ....

....

21 Choose 3 activities from Exercise 19 where you circled *occasionally* or *never*. Say how and when you will do each one in the furure.

Example: I will order videos and DVDs from the Internet or ask friends for them. I will watch them for 90 minutes a week.

Test your knowledge

22 Which of the following sentences are written in correct English? Put a tick (✓) or a cross (✗) in the brackets.

a Mobile phones are much cheaper than they used to be. [ ]
b My brother is not as old than me. [ ]
c I love modern music; the louder the best. [ ]
d What kind of holiday are you interested in? [ ]
e What about going somewhere in Hungary? [ ]
f If it was me, I'd go somewhere with more sun. [ ]
g One of the most good films I have ever seen is *Casablanca*. [ ]
h I prefer somewhere off the beaten track. [ ]
i The best holiday I've ever been on was a package holiday. [ ]
j It's getting more and more hotter every day. [ ]

Rewrite the items which you marked with a cross, to make correct sentences.

The phonemic alphabet

23 Consult the table of phonemic symbols on page 123 and then write these words and phrases in ordinary spelling.

a /ˈsaɪtsiːjɪŋ/ ....

b /ˌpækɪdʒˈhɒlɪdeɪ/ ....

c /ˈwɔːtəskiːjɪŋ/ ....

d /ˈbækpækəlænd/ ....

e /ɪgˈzɒtɪk/ ....

f /ʌnˈkʌmftəbəl/ ....

g /ɒfðəˌbiːtənˈtræk/ ....

Listen to Track 12 and check your answers.

Reading

1 Read the following poem, 'The Confession'. What is the correct order of the three verses. Write the numbers 1–3 in the brackets.

The Confession
by Brian Patten

When he showed her the photograph again,
she said,

[ ] 'It was a July afternoon.
The day was hot and my body hummed.
I was bored and in search of an adventure
That seemed beyond you.

[ ] 'Yes, I remember taking it.
I was incredibly young then.
You handed me the camera
And telling me over and over how to use it
You posed, smiling stiffly.
You were so pompous, so blind to everything.

[ ] 'Yet how can I forget that day?
Look closer at the photograph.
See there in the background,
In the corner behind you
The other boy, grinning so openly.'

2 Make sure you know the meaning of the words in the box below and then use them to complete the poem.

> clothes ◆ clumsily ◆ inside ◆ nothing ◆
> patiently ◆ poor ◆ smirks ◆ wearing

I Am Completely Different
by Karoda Saburo

I am completely different.
Though I am (**a**) .... the same tie as yesterday,
am as (**b**) .... as yesterday,
as good for (**c**) .... as yesterday,
today
I am completely different.
Though I am wearing the same (**d**) ....,
am as drunk as yesterday,
living as (**e**) .... as yesterday, nevertheless
today
I am completely different.

Ah –
I (**f**) .... close my eyes
on all the grins and (**g**) ....
on all the twisted smiles and horse laughs –
and glimpse then, (**h**) .... me,
one beautiful white butterfly
fluttering towards tomorrow.

3 Tick the correct column for each of the questions below.

Which poem:	'The Confession'	'I Am Completely Different'
a ... talks about clothes?		
b ... talks about an incident in the past?		
c ... has three people in it?		
d ... is written by a poet talking about himself or herself?		
e ... is more optimistic than pessimistic?		
f ... is about a long-kept secret?		
g ... talks about two people smiling very differently?		
h ... do you like best?		

Grammar: the present perfect

4 Read the information about Rita and Tom Redfern and write questions for the answers, using the present perfect. The first one is done for you.

Rita and Tom Redfern live in California, USA. Tom's a guitarist in a band called Moondance and Rita works for a recording company called Halcyon Music. Here are some facts about them.

- They moved to America a year ago.
- They bought their beach house last January.
- Rita started working for Halcyon Music last Monday.
- Tom started playing the guitar at the age of eight.
- Rita started her Japanese study classes six months ago.
- Tom joined a band called 'Moondance' nine months ago.

a 'How long have they lived in America ?' 'For 12 months.'
b '..?' 'Since January.'
c '..?' 'Since Monday.'
d '..?' 'Since he was eight.'
e '..?' 'For six months.'
f '..?' 'For nine months.'

5 Rewrite the sentences and questions using the present perfect and the words in brackets.

a I haven't been to the USA yet. (never)

I've never been to the USA.

b I had my last holiday two years ago. (for)

....

c I met the writer CJ Stone a few minutes ago. (just) ....

d I saw a beautiful camper van two minutes ago. (just)..

e I started living on a houseboat six months ago – and I still do. (for) ....

f I'm going to drive my new camper van soon. (yet)...

g Spending the night in a tent would be a completely new experience for me. (never)

....

h The last time I lived in a house was a year ago. (since)..

i The last time I was in the USA was in 2000. (since)..

j They'll finish building the house one day – I hope. (yet) ....

k Is this your first experience of sleeping in the open air? (ever) ....

6 Read the sentences. Write the correct past simple or present perfect form in the gaps. Use the words in brackets. The first one is done for you.

a I (live) ...*have lived*... in many strange places in my life and I (like) ....*liked*........ all of them – except for the houseboat!

b I (once/live) .... in a houseboat but it (sink) .... in the middle of the night. Luckily I (not-be) .... at home, but since then I (be) .... very suspicious of any kind of boat, so I (never/feel)........................... like trying a houseboat again.

c Once when I (be) .... in a tent on the edge of the desert, I (hear) .... a terrible roar in the night. I (be) .... terribly afraid, but I (never/be) .... able to find out what the animal was.

d I (always/want) .... to live at the top of a tall apartment block. I (have) .... a flat for about four years, but it (be) .... in the basement and I (not/like) .... that.

e I (drive) .... thousands of miles in my old camper van over the years, but when it (break down) .... last year, I (put) .... it in the garage and I (not/use) .... it since.

f I (sleep) .... in the open air on many occasions and I (always/enjoy) .... it, although I (not/like) .... it one night last summer when there (be) .... a fantastic storm and I (get) .... completely soaked and cold.

g I (be) .... in my present house for the last six months. I (move) .... here to be near my daughter.

Vocabulary: homes and houses

7 Draw a picture of a house and its surroundings with the following items clearly visible. Write the words next to the items.

basement ◆ camper van ◆ fence ◆ first floor ◆
garage ◆ garden ◆ gate ◆ ground floor ◆
semi-detached house ◆ tent

What other word labels can you add to your picture?

8 Unscramble the letters to make different types of living space, and then complete the table by ticking the appropriate columns. The first one is done for you. (If you are having trouble, look at Activities 2 and 17 in Unit 5 of the Student's Book.)

	can be moved	can be on the 25th floor	cramped	dark	is pretty cheap	light	more than one room	most like where I live	only has one floor/storey	part of a bigger building	spacious
a b g l n o u w						✓	✓		✓		
a c e m p r a n v											
a f l t											
a b e e m n s t a f l t											
e h o s u											
a b e h s t o o u											
b e i l m o e h m o											
e n o p i r a											
e n t t											

Listening

9 Listen to Track 13 and number the pictures (a – e) in the order in which they are talked about.

bathroom a ....

living room b ....

second bedroom c ....

main bedroom d ....

kitchen e ....

10 Which room:

a ... doesn't have space for much furniture?

....

b ... is nice to look out of (and isn't a bedroom)?

....

c ... can always be made warm?

....

d ... do they both like a lot?

....

e ... has some interesting furniture?

....

f ... could be either for sleeping or working?

....

g ... doesn't get any light from outside?

....

11 Answer these questions.

a How long has the house been empty?

....

b Why did the last tenants leave the house?

....

c What is Paul doing at the moment?

....

d What does Hilary do normally?

....

e What is she doing at the moment?

....

f What is the final decision about the house, and who makes it? ....

(To find out how Paul and Hilary got on in their new house, look at the 'Listening' section in Unit 6 of the Workbook.)

Functional language: welcoming people

12 Rearrange the words and punctuation to make appropriate sentences and questions.

a coming / . / for / Thanks
Thanks for coming.

b I / get / drink / ? / you / something / Can / to

....

c trouble / ? / you / here / any / finding / have / your / Did / way..

d ? / take / coat / Can / your / I

....

e Do / ? / up / to / need / you / freshen

....

f you / . / nice / to / How / see

....

g bad / . / , / lost / bit / got / a / but / too / it / wasn't / We ....

h ? / Yes / . / you / Have / an / got / orange / juice / please ....

i ? / bathroom / Can / is / me / tell / the / where / you ....

j great / you / to / . / It's / see

....

k , / I'll / if / it / all / I / on / No / right / . / think / keep / that's /. ....

13 Match the sentences and questions from Exercise 12 with these replies. The first one is done for you.

a 'Can I get you something to drink?'
'Yes, please. I'd love an apple juice, if you've got one.'

b '...'
'Yes, please. It's quite warm in here.'

c '...'
'No. Your directions were absolutely perfect.'

d '...'
'Yes please. I'd like to wash my hands.'

e '...'
'It's nice to see you too.'

f '...'
'Great to see you too.'

g '...'
'Why? It's not cold in here.'

h '...'
'Well, at least you're here now.'

i '...'
'No, I'm afraid not. But we've got mango juice or apple juice.'

j '...'
'It's just along the corridor. Last door on the right.'

14 Look at the different parts of a letter in the column on the left. Write the appropriate letter (*a – i*) in the diagram on the right. Sometimes more than one letter is possible.

a Yours sincerely
b Jenny Cook
c Dear Mr Greenfell
d April 4, 2002
e 33 Abbey Walk,
  Britley,
  Cambs CB1 8XJ
f Thank you for your letter ...
g I look forward to hearing from you.
h *Jenny Cook*

15 Read the following three letters. They have different levels of formality. Write the phrases in the correct places in the letters.

Dear Jill,
Dear Miss Brulo,
Hi Jane,
I enjoyed our meeting.
I look forward to hearing from you.

I'll wait to hear from you.
It was a pleasure to meet you.
So that's all OK.
With best wishes,
Yours sincerely,

1

1

2

3

4

5

6

7

8

1

(a) ....

Thank you very much for coming to see me yesterday.

(b) ....

Since you left I have talked to my colleagues and we have agreed that there is no reason why you should not use the library in our college for your research. However, as I mentioned in our discussion, we will need a letter from your own college confirming the subject of that research.

I hope this is acceptable, and (c) ....

(d) ....

Dr G Zephaniah
College librarian

2

(e) ....
Great to see you yesterday.
The people here say fine.
No Problems.
          Great!
(f) ....

Best,
Gerry

3

(g) ....
Thanks for coming in yesterday.

(h) ....

I've talked to the others and they say 'yes', so the next move is up to you (the letter from your college etc).

(i) ....

(j) ....

Kim

Which letter is the most formal: *1, 2* or *3*?

Pronunciation: stress

16 Listen to Track 14 and circle the two stressed syllables in these sentences. Put a line under the syllable with the biggest stress.

a It's great to see you.
b Oh, this is great!
c Can I take your coat?
d It's a bit cramped in here.
e I've just won a prize.
f Can I get you something to drink?
g Thanks for inviting us.

Listen to Track 14 again and repeat the phrases.

REFLECTIONS

Thinking about learning and language: speaking

17 What do you find difficult when you speak in English? Give each of the following a score from *0* (= *very easy*) to *5* (= *very difficult*). Put one more difficult thing in the last row.

Topic	Score
Pronunciation of individual words	
Finding the right words to use	
Speaking quickly	
Getting the grammar right	
(Something else – you choose an extra difficult thing, if you have one.)	

18 Here are some suggestions for practising speaking in English. Give them each a score from *1* (= *a good idea - I probably will do it*) to *3* (= *an excellent idea - I definitely will do it*). Put one more suggestion of your own in the last row.

Suggestion	Score
Go out with my classmates once a week and only speak English for, say, an hour.	
Listen to Audiotracks from *Just Right* and practise speaking in the same way as the people on the tracks.	
Practise saying difficult words and phrases to myself before trying them out in real life.	
Record myself saying words with difficult pronunciations.	
Send taped 'letters' to English-speaking friends or classmates.	
Speak in English without worrying too much about making mistakes.	
Write down new spoken phrases I hear (in class/ on the radio/on the Internet) and practise saying them to myself.	
(Your own suggestion)	

Test your knowledge

19 Translate the following sentences and questions.

a It's really cluttered in this room.

....

b It's time to make a decision.

....

c He's lived in a camper van for five years.

....

d Have you ever slept in a tent?

....

e When I'm away from home I feel really homesick.

....

f Did you have any trouble finding us?

....

g Where's the bathroom?

....

h I've just had an idea.

....

The phonemic alphabet

20 Consult the table of phonemic symbols on page 123 and then write these words and phrases in ordinary spelling.

a /'həʊmləs/.................................

b /'speɪʃəs/.................................

c /'bʌŋgələʊ/.................................

d /'gærɑːʒ/.................................

e /ðiːjˌəʊpən'eə/.................................

f /ˌblɒkəv'flæts/.................................

g /ˌθeŋksfə'kʌmɪŋ/.................................

Listen to Track 15 and check your answers.

Vocabulary: different histories

1 Look at the circled word. Can you find sixteen more words used to talk about history, biography and crime in the puzzle?

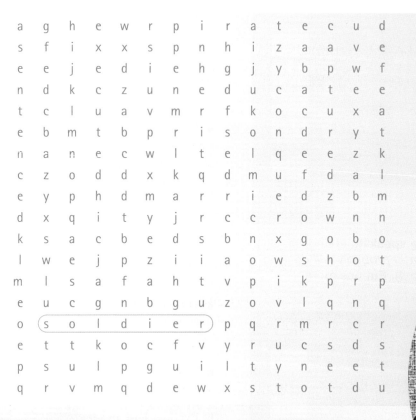

```
a  g  h  e  w  r  p  i  r  a  t  e  c  u  d
s  f  i  x  x  s  p  n  h  i  z  a  a  v  e
e  e  j  e  d  i  e  h  g  j  y  b  p  w  f
n  d  k  c  z  u  n  e  d  u  c  a  t  e  e
t  c  l  u  a  v  m  r  f  k  o  c  u  x  a
e  b  m  t  b  p  r  i  s  o  n  d  r  y  t
ñ  a  n  e  c  w  l  t  e  l  q  e  e  z  k
c  z  o  d  d  x  k  q  d  m  u  f  d  a  l
e  y  p  h  d  m  a  r  r  i  e  d  z  b  m
d  x  q  i  t  y  j  r  c  c  r  o  w  n  n
k  s  a  c  b  e  d  s  b  n  x  g  o  b  o
l  w  e  j  p  z  i  i  a  o  w  s  h  o  t
m  l  s  a  f  a  h  t  v  p  i  k  p  r  p
e  u  c  g  n  b  g  u  z  o  v  l  q  n  q
o (s  o  l  d  i  e  r) p  q  r  m  r  c  r
e  t  t  k  o  c  f  v  y  r  u  c  s  d  s
p  s  u  l  p  g  u  i  l  t  y  n  e  e  t
q  r  v  m  q  d  e  w  x  s  t  o  t  d  u
```

2 Use words from the puzzle in the following text (you may have to change the form of some of the verbs). The first letter is given for each word. You need to use one of the words twice.

Benjamina Woolley was **(a)** b.................... in a small village in 1623. She was **(b)** e.................... at the local school, and at the age of twenty-six she **(c)** i.................... a lot of money from an uncle she had never met. She went to London and **(d)** m.................... a rich banker. But the marriage was not a success and one night she **(e)** p.................... him. She was sent to **(f)** p...................., but she **(g)** e...................., disguised as a **(h)** s.................... .

Benjamina went to the West Indies where she met and married the **(i)** p...................., Bill Scarface. They sailed the oceans and **(j)** c.................... many ships. But the marriage didn't work, so she **(k)** d.................... the pirate and went to live in America. There she **(l)** m.................... three more times, but in the end, after she **(m)** s.................... her fifth husband during a card game, she was **(n)** e..................... She was 125 years old.

Do you believe the story? Why?

....
....
....
....
....
....
....
....

3 Read the information about Henry VIII. Put his wives in chronological order, that is to say, the order in which they were his wives. The following rhyme, which British school children used to learn, may help you.

Divorced, beheaded, died

Divorced, beheaded, survived.

1 ....
2 ....
3 ....
4 ....
5 ....
6 ....

Do not marry this man!

Being married to England's King Henry VIII was a dangerous business. It could easily cost you your life!

Henry VIII (1491–1547) is one of the most famous characters in English history. As a young man he was handsome and extremely athletic, and according to contemporary accounts, everyone thought he was extremely attractive. He was a brilliant horseman, and a superb shot with a bow and arrow. He was expert at an early version of the game of tennis, and was also an accomplished musician. The famous tune 'Greensleeves' is said to have been written by him, though there is no proof of this.

The one thing Henry was not very good at was having sons. He married six different women to try and produce a male heir to the throne, but his only son from all these marriages died when he was just 16 years old. However, his two daughters both became queens of England, so if he had only lived long enough, he might not have been so worried. In alphabetical order, Henry's six wives were as follows.

Anne Boleyn (1507–36)

Henry fell in love with her when he was still married to his first wife, Catherine of Aragon. Catherine had failed to give him a son, so he divorced her to marry Anne. Anne had a daughter called Elizabeth (who later became Queen Elizabeth I) but no son. When Henry got tired of her, they found a reason to accuse her of crimes against the king. She was found guilty and executed by having her head cut off.

Anne of Cleves (1515–57)

After Jane Seymour's death Henry was extremely unhappy. But an artist brought him back a portrait of Anne of Cleves. She seemed very good-looking, and marriage to her was good politics. But when Henry saw her, he thought she was ugly and never liked her. They were married for less than a year before Henry divorced her.

Catherine of Aragon (1485–1536)

Daughter of Ferdinand V of Castile (Spain). She married Arthur, eldest son of Henry VII of England, but when he died she married his brother Henry VIII. She had one daughter (Mary) who later became queen of England before her half-sister Elizabeth. However Catherine had no sons so Henry divorced her to marry Anne Boleyn, a woman he'd fallen in love with.

Catherine Howard (1521–42)

Catherine Howard was the niece of the Duke of Norfolk, one of the most important men in the country after the king. She was married to Henry in 1540, just after his disastrous marriage to Anne of Cleves. But less than two years later Catherine was accused of loving someone else and was executed.

Catherine Parr (1512–48)

Henry's last wife was the one, people said, who could best control the old king. She was sweet and kind, and Henry, who was by now ill and fat, loved her in his own way. Catherine was still alive when Henry died. She remarried but died in childbirth a year later.

Jane Seymour (1509–37)

Henry fell in love with Jane Seymour while he was still married to Anne Boleyn. As soon as Anne had been executed he married Jane and in 1537, a year later, she produced a son, Edward VI, but died herself 12 days later. On the death of Henry, Edward became king at the age of nine, but died six years later.

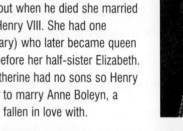

4 **Look at the way the following words and phrases are used in the text on page 43 and then write them in the gaps in the sentences.**

a A boy who will become king after the present king dies is his

....

b A piece of information that shows beyond doubt that something

is true is called ....

c Historians talk about things written at the same time as they

happened as ....

d If you want someone to do exactly what you tell them and only

what you tell them, you will try to .... them.

e My brother's daughter is my ....

f When someone can hit a target every time (with a gun or a bow

and arrow), we call them a ....

g When a woman dies at the same time as her baby is born, we say

she ....

h When somebody is very good and experienced at something, they

are called ....

i When someone is very good at physical sports, we often call

them ....

j When someone makes a decision that will help them or their

country, we can say that it is ....

k When something is a complete failure, we call it ....

l A man who regularly rides a horse is called a ....

accomplished

athletic

contemporary accounts

control

died in childbirth

disastrous

good politics

horseman

niece

male heir

proof

superb shot

5 **Complete the following table with the information required.**

a Any three things Henry was good at:	1 ....
	2 ....
	3 ....
b The names of Henry's children in order of birth:	1 ....
	2 ....
	3 ....
c Write the names of Henry's children in the order that they were king or queen:	1 ....
	2 ....
	3 ....
d The name of the wife who lived the longest:	....
e The name of the wife who had a son:	....
f The name of the wife who Henry thought was ugly:	....
g The name of the wife married to Henry's brother:	....

Grammar: the passive

6 Complete each gap with one of the following verbs. Decide if they should be active or passive. The first two are done for you.

> agree ◆ appoint ◆ behead ◆ change ◆ convict ◆ die ◆ educate ◆ enter ◆ imprison ◆ knight ◆ know ◆ make (x2) ◆ release ◆ resign ◆ start ◆ write ◆ summon

A Man for All Seasons is a film that tells the story of Sir Thomas More.

Thomas More was born in London on 7 February 1478. He (**a**) _was educated_ at the University of Oxford, and in 1504 he (**b**) _entered_ Parliament. However, he spoke out against the king (Henry VII) and, because of this, More's father (**c**) .... He (**d**) (not) .... until Thomas More, his son, agreed to leave public life.

After Henry VII died and his son, Henry VIII, became king, More entered public life again. He (**e**) .... in 1521 and became 'Sir Thomas More'. He (**f**) .... speaker (chief official) of the House of Commons, England's parliament.

During this period, Sir Thomas More was close to the king. They frequently had long and enjoyable conversations and in 1529 Sir Thomas More (**g**) .... Lord Chancellor of England by his friend the king. The Lord Chancellor is the chief law official in the country.

Trouble (**h**) .... when Henry VIII wanted to divorce his first wife, Catherine of Aragon. More (**i**) (not) .... with this because of his religious beliefs and so he (**j**) .... from public life (again) in 1532. But this was not enough for the king. He was desperate for More's approval. But Sir Thomas would not (**k**) .... his mind. The king was furious and, as a result, Sir Thomas More (**l**) .... to court and (**m**) .... of treason, a serious crime against the king and the state. He (**n**) .... on 7 July 1535. Four hundred years later, he (**o**) .... a saint by the Catholic church because he (**p**) .... for his beliefs.

Sir Thomas (**q**) (also) .... for his book *Utopia*, which (**r**) .... in 1516.

7 Look at the phrases on the left and make a passive sentence. Start your sentence with the words in blue, and make the verb in brackets passive, as in the example. You may need to add *by* before the agent.

a Millions of emails around the world every day (send)

Millions of emails are sent around the world every day.

b The *Mona Lisa* a few people every day (photograph)

....
....
....

c *Cats,* the musical more people than any other musical (see)

....
....
....

d Heathrow Airport 1.5 million people every year (use)

....
....
....

e Machu Picchu 68,000 people since last January (visit)

....
....
....

f Mount Everest teams from all over the world every year (climb)

....
....
....

g The *Vendée Globe* round-the-world yacht race a woman never (win)

....
....
....

h The Great Wall of China astronauts in space (see)

....
....

◀))◔ 8 Listen to Track 16. Number these events in the order you hear them on the track.

a A strange voice is heard. [   ]

b Hilary stops speaking. [   ]

c Jane gets really frightened. [   ]

d Mark leaves the room. [   ]

e Paul leaves the room. [   ]

f The lights go out. [   ]

9 Listen to Track 16 again. Are these statements *True*, *False* or *Possible*? Write *T*, *F* or *P* in the brackets

a At the start of the conversation Hilary is happy in the house. [   ]

b Mark believes in ghosts. [   ]

c People say that a family was murdered in the house. [   ]

d The weather is the same as it was 300 years ago when two strangers knocked at the door. [   ]

e Paul and Hilary cry 'strangers, strangers' on cold nights. [   ]

f The electricity stops working in the house from time to time. [   ]

g There are some candles in the house. [   ]

h Somebody knocks at the door. [   ]

i It's warmer in the room at the end of the conversation than it was at the beginning. [   ]

j There are ghosts in the house. [   ]

10 Complete these extracts from Track 16 with one word or expression for each gap.

JANE: So, do you like (a) .... here Hilary?

HILARY: Yes. It's a great (b) .... to rent while Paul is (c) .... his novel. But I wouldn't like to live here for (d) ....

PAUL: It's got ghosts, apparently.

MARK: Oh (e) .... be silly. Nobody believes in (f) ....

PAUL: Why not, Mark?

MARK: Paul! You're a rational (g) .... being. You can't believe all that stuff.

JANE: What's the story, then, (h) .... this place? Why does it have ghosts?

JANE: What was that?

PAUL: Oh no! Not (i) .... The electricity. I wonder how long we'll be (j) .... light this time.

MARK: Do you have (k) .... candles?

HILARY: Not sure. Have we got (l) .... left?

PAUL: I (m) .... so. I (n) .... where they are. (o) .... go.

HILARY: Thanks, Paul.

JANE: What was (p) .... ?

HILARY: What was (q) .... ?

JANE: That noise.

HILARY: I didn't hear a (r) ....

Functional language: paying compliments

11 Put in a line to show the beginnings and ends of the words in the word chain. The first one is done for you.

silk|polyestercottonleatherplasticwoolcorduroynylondenim

Choose six words from the list to match the pictures.

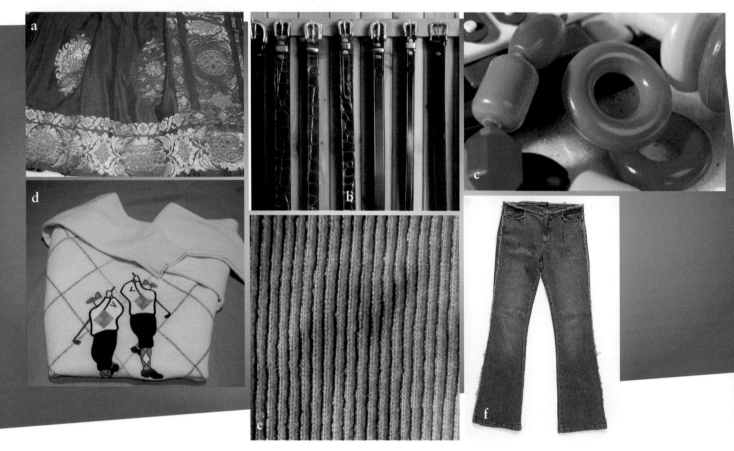

12 Complete the conversations with the lines from the box.

It was a present from my husband.

It was given to me by my aunt.

No, I don't think so. It's from Korea.

Oh thanks.

Oh yes. So it's a Swiss watch then?

Well it looks good with that suit.

What's it made of?

Where did you get it?

a SUSAN: That's a really nice jacket.

MARY: (**1**) ....

SUSAN: Not at all! Where did you get it?

MARY: (**2**) ....

SUSAN: He chose well. It really suits you.

b RACHEL: I like your shirt.

TOM: (**1**) ....

RACHEL: (**2**) ....

(**3**) ....

TOM: I don't know. Cotton, I expect.

c BILL: That's a really nice watch.

GRAHAM: I'm glad you like it.

BILL: (**1**) ....

GRAHAM: From that shop in Constitution Square, you know, the one opposite the cinema.

BILL: (**2**) ....

GRAHAM: (**3**) ....

Writing: mini-biographies

13 Use the notes in boxes *a – c* to write three paragraphs about the saxophonist Barbara Thompson in the spaces provided below.

> a 1 Known as a quiet person (among her friends)
> 2 Not the typical jazz lifestyle of late nights and crazy living
> 3 'It's only when she's on stage that she really lights up. Then she changes completely. Her whole personality changes completely.' (David – husband and manager)

> b 1 Name: Barbara Thompson
> 2 Born: 1954, in Manchester, UK
> 3 Father: scientist
> 4 Mother: history teacher
> 5 No musicians in family
> 6. Started learning to play the saxophone at secondary school

> c • Became ill.
> • Last concert in 2001.
> • 'I can't play like I used to, so there's no point in asking people to pay to come and see me.' (Thompson)
> • Current activities: writing music; teaching younger players

Paragraph 1:
Introduce the person, their background, and early events.

Paragraph 2:
Describe the person and their interests.

Paragraph 3:
Talk about the most recent events in their life and discuss what they are doing now or in the future.

Pronunciation: intonation clues

14 Are these statements or questions? Listen to Track 17 and put a full stop (.) or question mark (?) at the end of each phrase. The first two are done for you.

a She inherited a million dollars **?**

b She inherited a million dollars **.**

c A million dollars

d A million dollars

e You like spaghetti

f You like spaghetti

g Yes

h Yes

i He was given a prize

j He was given a prize

k They really suit me

l They really suit me

Listen to Track 17 again and repeat the phrases.

REFLECTIONS

Thinking about learning and language: writing

15 Which of the following do you/will you write in English? Choose your top five and complete the 'Type of writing' column in the table in order of priority where *1 = most important, 2 = next most important*, etc.

> diary ◆ emails ◆ essays ◆ faxes ◆ forms ◆ instructions ◆ letters ◆ lists ◆ memos ◆ poems ◆ postcards ◆ reports ◆ stories ◆ study notes

Priority number	Type of writing	Difficulty level
1		
2		
3		
4		
5		

Now number your top five in order of difficulty. Put *1 (= most difficult)* to *5 (= least difficult)* in the right-hand column.

16 Find an example of one of your top five in the Student's Book or from some other source. Analyse the writing by answering the following questions.

a Who is it written by? ....

b Who is it written for? ....

c What does the writer want to achieve? ....

d What structure does the writing have (paragraphs, greetings, headings, etc)? ....

e What special words and expressions are used? ....

....

Test your knowledge

17 Which of the following sentences are written in correct English? Put a tick (✓) or a cross (✗) in the brackets. If there is an error, correct it.

a He was education in London. [ ]
b Was he disguised as a soldier? [ ]
c He was sent to prison for five years. [ ]
d Much of my surprise I arrived on time. [ ]
e Raw fish is eating in Japan. [ ]
f He was given for literature a prize. [ ]
g Kai Tek airport was designed by Norman Foster. [ ]
h Don't interrupt me. I have a lot on my mind. [ ]
i That jacket looks good in you. [ ]
j That's a really nice earrings. [ ]

Rewrite the items which you marked with a cross to make correct sentences.

The phonemic alphabet

18 Consult the table of phonemic symbols on page 123 and then write these words and phrases in ordinary spelling.

a /ˈkɒŋkəd/ ....

b /ˈeksəkuːtɪd/ ....

c /dɪsˈgaɪzd/ ....

d /ˈkɔːdərɔɪ/ ....

e /ˈleðə/ ....

f /ˌhauˈɪntrəstɪŋ/ ....

g /aɪdəˈnəu/ ....

Listen to Track 18 and check your answers.

UNIT 7 Good intentions

Grammar: the future

1 Complete the following sentences with one word for each gap. The first letter is given in each case.

a We are g............... to see a film tonight.

b I don't feel very well. I think I'm going t............... faint.

c We're m............... them outside the cinema at eight.

d If I can afford it, I think I'll v............... my sister in Mexico next summer.

e According to the weather forecast it is going to r............... later on today.

f Sit down and relax. I'll m............... you a nice cup of tea.

g According to the guide book the museum c............... today at 4.30.

h Who's g............... to give her the bad news? I don't have the nerve.

i I'll p............... never see her again!

2 Use *will* or *going to* or the present continuous, and the words in brackets, to complete these sentences and questions. If two answers are possible, write the one that seems the best. The first one is done for you.

a Thank you so much for your kindness. I'll always remember it. (always/ remember)

b You .... sorry that you said that. Just you wait and see! (be)

c I .... television in a minute – there's a programme I want to see. I .... back after the programme. (watch; ring)

d .... you .... me some money? I seem to have run out. (lend)

e I .... you in half an hour. I .... a shower first. (see; have)

f She says that she .... him again. (never/see)

3 Choose the most appropriate verb form (*will*, *be going to*, present continuous or present simple) for the words in brackets in this conversation. The first one is done for you.

HELENA: (**a.** we/be) Are we going to be in time?

SUSIE: Yes, I think so.

HELENA: What time (**b.** the train/arrive) ....?

SUSIE: At 8.15. Oh no, wait a minute, look, there's a delay. It (**c.** not/get in) .... until nine o'clock.

HELENA: What (**d.** we/do) .... until then?

SUSIE: I don't know.

HELENA: Well, I (**e.** get) .... a coffee. Do you want one?

SUSIE: No, but I (**f.** come) .... to the cafeteria with you.

HELENA: What (**g.** you/say) .... to him when you see him?

SUSIE: I don't really know. I mean I can't think of anything to say.

HELENA: Don't worry. I (**h.** do) .... the talking.

SUSIE: OK. I (**i.** just/stand) .... and listen.

HELENA: I don't believe that for a moment.

SUSIE: Well, I (**j.** not/shout) .... at him or anything. Just because he said he'd catch an earlier train. I mean he's nearly 17.

HELENA: What (**k.** he/do) .... when he leaves school?

SUSIE: I wish I knew. He (**l.** probably/go) .... travelling with his friends. That's what they all seem to do.

HELENA: (**m.** you/miss) .... him?

SUSIE: Yes, I think so. It (**n.** feel) .... very strange with no one in the house except for me and the dog.

4 Write the phrasal verbs from the box in the correct rows. Some will go in more than one row.

break up with ◆ cut down on ◆ get round to ◆ give up ◆ go on ◆ look after ◆ make a go of ◆ pick up ◆ put in ◆ run out of ◆ see about ◆ set up ◆ take off ◆ take up

a Phrasal verbs which can be used with no object (e.g. *set off*, *slow down*)

b Phrasal verbs which can be followed by an object (e.g. *cut up something*, *run over something*)

c Phrasal verbs which can have an object between the verb and the particle (e.g. *cut something up*, *look it up*)

5 Choose nine of the phrasal verbs from Exercise 4 to complete this text. Be careful to use the correct tense each time.

JULIO'S DILEMMA

Six months ago Julio Gonzalez and his sister Marcia both worked for a car company. They were both fed up with their jobs, and then Marcia (a) .... her boyfriend of three years – and started to feel very unhappy. She needed something to make her feel better, so one day she said to her brother, 'Look, I can't (b) .... working in a boring job, and I don't like feeling unhappy. I want to do something new. Let's start our own business. I'm sure we could (c) .... it if we worked hard.'

And so they (d) .... a car repair business. At first everything went well. Julio (e) .... about 60 hours a week. Occasionally he would (f) .... seeing a film with his wife or going out for a drink with his friend Hedley, and that was about all. It was just

work, work, work. But then one day, after a conversation with his friend, he (g) .... golf – and now he spends more and more time at the golf course.

His sister and wife are both furious. 'With you it's either work or golf! What kind of a life is that?' his wife complained to him last night. 'If you don't (h) .... one or the other, I'm going to go on strike, and you can run this house and this family by yourself. See how you like that!'

Julio's sister is just as dramatic.

(i) '............................ golf,' she told him yesterday. 'We've got a factory to run!'

So that's Julio's dilemma. Work, golf, his wife and his sister. As he said to his friend Hedley, 'What am I going to do?'

6 Read the newspaper article, and then write the correct names under the pictures below.

a .... b ....

c .... d ....

Marathon marriage just the tip of the iceberg

When Angela Stratford agreed to marry Nigel Jones, they decided to do it in style. They're just one of the many couples who choose an out-of-the-ordinary experience for the most important day in their lives.

Nigel Jones, 48, and his 34-year-old wife Angela had been together for six years before they became husband and wife in 2001. They ran hand in hand for 25 miles of the 2001 London marathon before stopping at a statue called Cleopatra's Needle, where family and friends cheered as they were married. After the ceremony they ran the last mile of the race waving a banner that said 'Just Married'. Later they had a wedding reception at a hotel in Greenwich.

Angela met Nigel at a running club – and thought of the marathon wedding. 'I just thought it was the perfect way to get married,' she said. But she only agreed to become Nigel's wife when he could run as fast as she could. 'I said only a man who can catch me will be able to marry me,' she said. 'He ran and ran, and eventually got to my level, and we started doing races together. I wasn't interested in anyone who didn't want to race!'

The bride wore a knee-length cream wedding dress with veil and cream gloves. Her husband-to-be wore shorts, a jacket and a pretend shirt and tie.

Bishop Jonathan Blake who conducted the wedding ceremony said, 'I have married people underwater, over the Internet, on boats and aeroplanes. I think it is wonderful that people can be free to express themselves, choose a service and an interesting setting that has more meaning for them. But I can't imagine getting married after running 25 miles.'

But if you don't fancy running a marathon to get married, you could always decide to go abroad for that special day and travel companies are now doing their best to persuade young couples to do just that. 'With the average cost of a wedding in the UK being about £12,000,' according to Sasha Pliotnov, a designer who specialises in marriage ceremonies, 'quite a few people are beginning to realise that it's a lot cheaper to fly off with just a few special friends and family to some exotic location and get married on a beautiful island or in some other romantic setting.'

There is no limit to the number and type of locations on offer. Award-winning tour operator *Kuoni*, for example, advertises 24 different packages. Its most popular one is the Triton Hotel in Sri Lanka. *Thomson Cruises* suggests a wedding on board ship – and you don't even have to travel far for the honeymoon. *Sandals Luxury Resorts* offer all sorts of wedding packages in the Caribbean, and *My Travel Group* offers anything from an Austrian chapel to the Australian outback.

Of course if you don't want to go abroad, you could always get married in a hot air balloon, on an ice-skating rink, up a mountain, or in a tree. They've all been done.

None of this impresses Ronald and Daisy Crabtree who got married on the same day as Nigel and Angela's interrupted marathon wedding. 'We got married in church,' Roger said, 'because that's the tradition. Daisy wore a traditional wedding dress and I wore a morning coat and a top hat. That's how people have always got married and it seemed the right thing for us too. We had a lovely day, something we will always remember.'

7 According to the text, who:

a ... completed a race after they were married?

....

b ... encourages people to get married on a boat?

....

c ... got married after the man answered a challenge successfully?

....

d ... has been an official at many strange weddings? ....

e ... knows the price of weddings?

....

f ... met in 1995?

....

g ... offers weddings in Austria?

....

h ... wants people to get married in Sri Lanka?

....

i ... will always remember their wedding?

....

j ... wore a traditional wedding dress?

....

8 Look at the way the phrases in the box are used in the text and then use them to fill the gaps in these sentences.

> exotic location ◆ got to my level ◆ hand in hand ◆
> in style ◆ out of the ordinary ◆ romantic setting ◆
> the tip of an iceberg ◆ wedding package ◆
> wedding reception

a A location that makes people think of love or feel loving is sometimes described as a

....

b A phrase to describe a small part of a much bigger situation is ....

....

c An all-inclusive programme you pay for when you book your wedding through a travel agent can be called a ....

....

d An unusual, interesting and often foreign place can be referred to as an ....

....

e When he reached the same standard as me, he

....

f If something is very unusual or different, we say it is ....

g If you do something in a way that people admire and/or which costs a lot of money, you could say that you are doing it ....

....

h The party after two people are married is called a ....

i When two people hold each other's hand, we say they are ....

....

Functional language: making promises

9 Choose the appropriate ending from the box and write the second part of the following sentences (*a–j*). The first one is done for you.

... and obey you forever.

... be there on time – for once!

... but I don't promise to make a particularly good job of it.

... but you have to organise the drinks.

... get to class late again. Honestly.

... if you'll do all the cooking.

... promise not to play such loud music in the evenings.

... rude to all my friends when I invite them round to our flat?

... the bathroom tidy, at least?

... you'll never misbehave in class again?

a Do you promise not to be _rude to all my friends when I invite them round to our flat?_

b I agree to give you more time to yourself, but you have to ....

....

c I give you my word that I'll never ....

....

d I promise that I'll ....

....

e I promise to love ....

....

f I'll get some glasses, ...

....

g Let's make a bargain. I'll do all the washing up

....

h Look, I'll agree to paint the walls in the kitchen

....

i Will you agree to keep ....

....

j Will you give me your word that ....

....

10 Complete the following diagram.

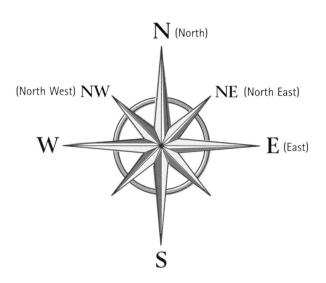

11 Match the terms (*a – g*) with the graphic symbols below.

a cloudy with sunny periods [   ]

b cloudy, light rain [   ]

c raining heavily [   ]

d heavy cloud [   ]

e snow [   ]

f heavy snow [   ]

g two degrees centigrade [   ]

12 Listen to Track 19 and answer the questions.

a What time of day is it? ....

b What is the warmest part of the country in the afternoon? ....

c What is the coldest part of the country in the afternoon? ....

d Where is Samantha going this afternoon?

....

13 Listen to Track 19 again, as many times as you want, and draw the symbols (in the box) on the maps. Include the temperature too (e.g. -1°C).

a Now

b Later today

c Tonight

d Tomorrow

14 Complete the following extract from Track 19 with one word for each gap.

Things aren't quite so bad in Wales and the west. Here the rain will gradually (**1**) .... away in the (**2**) .... afternoon, so people can expect (**3**) .... a dry night, though (**4**) .... looks (**5**) .... being a day of scattered showers.

Up the east (**6**) .... of the country, in the north, and (**7**) .... north into Scotland, it's pretty (**8**) .... already, as anyone there (**9**) .... It's about minus 2 (**10**) .... centigrade, with heavy (**11**) .... , but that should go (**12**).............................. to about one degree during the (**13**) .... But the outlook doesn't (**14**) .... good. Expect some snow by (**15**) .... , starting quite light, but gradually (**16**) .... so that by the evening it will be (**17**) .... , with blizzard-like conditions on the (**18**) .... , so do be careful. In fact the (**19**) .... have just issued advice to motorists not to (**20**) .... at all unless your journey is absolutely (**21**) .... Temperatures tonight will drop to about (**22**) .... 6 degrees.

And what of (**23**) .... ? As I said, in the (**24**) .... of the country, it's going to be wet and cloudy, scattered (**25**) .... with the occasional burst of heavier (**26**) .... In the north and east, (**27**) .... should settle in for a (**28**) .... spell with more snowfall over the (**29**) .... few days. Not quite so bad in the south and west, though. Here there will be some (**30**) .... – when it isn't raining, that is.

15 Complete the invitations using the phrases in the blue box. The invitations have different levels of formality, so be careful that you use the appropriate phrase each time.

> Bring this invite with ◆ have great pleasure in inviting you ◆ Hi Steve, ◆ in the history of the world ◆ let us know if you can come. ◆ RSVP ◆ would like to invite you ◆ You will come? Please?

Charlie & Matt

(a) ....
to their flat-warming party.
Date: Saturday August 7
Time: 7.30 pm onwards
Place: 36a Lark's Drive, Parkland
(b) ....
Tel: 0209 573 44445
email: charlie_p@justmail.com

The best 18th birthday party
(c) ....
Yes, that's right
Angela & Petra are both
18!
So come to the Q club -
8 till late.
(d) ....you.
(You'd be a fool to miss it.)

```
From: Ruth <ruthS@violabest.com>
To:   Stephen <SBeaumont@freenot.co.uk>
Cc:
Bcc:
Subject:  thinking of a party
(e) ...............................................
We're having a party on Saturday. Come along if
possible. OK?
All you'll need is a bottle; we'll provide the rest.
(f) ...............................................
Ruth
(I'd really appreciate it if you didn't tell Brian
about this......)
```

Richard and Barbara Hamilton
(g) .... *to a luncheon*
to celebrate their golden wedding anniversary
On June 22
12.30 for 1
The Groucho Club
London W1
(h) *Please* ....

16 Write the names.

Whose invitation:

a ... is the most formal? ....

b ... celebrates 50 years of being together? ....

c ... is because two people have just started to live in a new place?

....

d ... is from two people of the same age?.........................

e ... is the least formal?...

f ... is for a party just for fun (no special reason)? ....

17 Listen to this sentence said in different ways on Track 20. Underline the word that is stressed most strongly in each case.

a I promise I'll be at your house by four o'clock.

b I promise I'll be at your house by four o'clock.

c I promise I'll be at your house by four o'clock.

d I promise I'll be at your house by four o'clock.

e I promise I'll be at your house by four o'clock.

18 Listen to Track 20 again and match these meanings with the sentences in Exercise 17. The first one is done for you.

1 I don't know about anyone else. [d]

2 I really, really do promise. [ ]

3 I'm not going to anyone else's house. [ ]

4 Not at any other time – not later anyway. [ ]

5 Not at your office. [ ]

19 Listen Track 20 and repeat the sentences in the same way.

REFLECTIONS

Thinking about learning and language: guessing words

20 Study this table and complete the task which follows.

Part of speech	Description	Example words
noun	a word that is the name of a person, a place, a thing, an activity, a quality or an idea	*Tom* *telephone* *tennis*
adjective	a word that gives more information about a noun or pronoun	*big* *distant* *perfect*
verb	a word or phrase which is used in describing an action, experience or state	*answer* *take up* *promise*
adverb	a word that adds to the meaning of a verb, adjective, another adverb or a whole sentence	*quietly* *drastically* *hardly*

What is the word in blue? Write *noun*, *adjective*, *verb* or *adverb*.

a I'll see you tomorrow. ....

b Caroline's going to win the race. ....

c It's going to be a really incredible concert. ....

d I'll never forget you! ....

e She's fantastically beautiful. ....

f We're going to make a go of our new restaurant ....

g I'm going to stop missing school. ....

h There's going to be a large crowd at the wedding ....

21 When you meet a new word, first see if it is a noun, verb, etc. Put *N, V, ADJ* or *ADV* in the brackets after the nonsense word (*kiddle*).

I'll never forget New Year's Eve two years ago. We had a *kiddle* (**a** ....) party at Jay's house and everybody came – and quite a lot of *kiddles* (**b** ....) that nobody seemed to know at all! I guess they just walked in off the *kiddle* (**c** ....). It was a bit embarrassing actually. But soon everyone was *kiddling* (**d** ....), dancing *kiddly* (**e** ....) to the music and having a good time.

One of the *kiddles* (**f** ....) was a guy I thought I had seen before, so I *kiddled* (**g** ....) over to him and tried to have an intelligent *kiddle* (**h** ....). But it was no good. He seemed really unfriendly. Every time I said anything he just turned and looked *kiddly* (**i** ....) at me without *kiddling* (**j** ....) a word. But then, later in the evening, just as the clock struck twelve he *kiddled* (**k** ....) to me and asked my name.

What word could replace the nonsense word in each case?

Test your knowledge

22 Translate the following sentences and questions.

a I'm never going to eat another chocolate. ....

....

b It'll be midnight in about 30 seconds. ....

c Will somebody please answer the phone? ....

d I'm meeting him at four o'clock tomorrow afternoon.

....

e What's the matter? You look tired. ....

f Nobody's perfect! ....

g I promise to love you for ever.

....

h Mr and Mrs Smith have great pleasure in inviting you for dinner. ....

Did you have problems? If you did, go back to the relevant activity in the Student's Book to check on meaning and use.

The phonemic alphabet

23 Consult the table of phonemic symbols on page 123 and then write these words and phrases in ordinary spelling.

a /təˈmɒrəʊ/ ....

b /ˈwedɪŋ/ ....

c /rezəˈluːʃən/ ....

d /ˈfaɪəfaɪtə/ ....

e /ˌnjuːjɪəz ˈiːv/ ....

f /ˌnəʊbədɪzˈpɜːfekt/ ....

g /aɪˌkaːntˈkəʊp/ ....

Check your answers by listening to Track 21.

UNIT 8 You can't do that here!

Listening 🔊

1 Look at the pictures (*a–d*). Listen to Track 22. Number the pictures *1– 4* in the order you hear the scenes.

a [......]

b [......]

c [......]

d [......]

2 Complete the phrases from the conversations. Write which scene, (*a–d*) in Exercise 1, the phrases come from. The first one is done for you.

		Picture
a Can't you read ....*the sign*........... ?		[*b*]
b Could you turn .... ?		[ ]
c Have you just .... ?		[ ]
d I can't .... I .... can't.		[ ]
e It means you can't		[ ]
f It means you .... I suppose.		[ ]
g It's driving		[ ]
h What .... mean?		[ ]
i Will you please		[ ]

3 Answer the following questions with phrases such as 'the man in picture *a*', 'the girl in picture *d*', etc.

Who:

a ... stopped suddenly and dramatically?

....

b ... was upset by a voice?

....

c ... was upset by a sound?

....

d ... was embarrassed by a relation?

....

e ... was sarcastic?

....

f ... had to stop talking to someone?

....

g ... had to pick something up?

....

h ... had to move?

....

Vocabulary: anti-social activities

4   Find fourteen words or expressions in the word chain. Put a line between each word or expression. The first one is done for you.

alarm|barbecuebonfirefootpathgraffitiinventlibrarylittermobilephonepavementpostersignaturespraypaintwalkman

Check your answer in the key.

5   Using words from Exercise 4, and expressions from Activity 6 in Unit 7 of the Student's Book, write instructions with *don't* for the following signs. The first one has been done for you.

a   *Don't bring food into the library.*
b   ....
c   ....
d   ....

e   ....
f   ....
g   ....
h   ....

Grammar: present modals – obligation, recommendation & permission

6   Use the modal verbs in brackets to make sentences from the following words. Be careful when you have to make a question or a negative. The first one is done for you.

a   I/eat/my sandwich outside? (must) ..... *Must I eat my sandwich outside?* ....

b   I/get/here before 7 o'clock? (should) ....

c   you/have/identification to take books out of the library? (need to) ....

d   you/worry/about the washing up. (need not) ....

e   they/hurry up/the concert starts in ten minutes. (should) ....

f   she/take/the science exam? (have to) ....

g   they/spray-paint/any more walls. (had better not) ....

h   we/wear/smart clothes for your party? (need) ....

i   you/speak/to your brother like that. (ought not) ....

j   you/take/plants out of the country. (must not) ....

7 Circle the best alternative, in blue, in each sentence.

  a You shouldn't/oughtn't to/needn't wear smart clothes at the party. It's not necessary.

  b Travellers should/can't/have to show their passports to the immigration officials. It's the law.

  c People can't/needn't/oughtn't to smoke in here. It's not allowed.

  d She must/needn't/had better study harder. That's what I want her to do – because I want her to pass that exam.

  e You must/can't/needn't listen to what I have to say. I insist on it.

  f You don't need to/can't/mustn't study very hard. You're going to pass the exam anyway.

  g You can't/needn't/ought to be more careful – or you might get hurt.

  h They had better/can't/shouldn't hurry up if they want to catch the train.

  i Those people needn't/oughtn't to/had better make so much noise in here. People are trying to work.

  j I can't/mustn't/must remember to ring my mother before I go out.

8 Rewrite the following sentences using *should, must, have to, don't have to* or *can't*. Start each sentence with *You*.

  a Getting up early isn't necessary tomorrow.

  ....

  b Wearing a uniform is not compulsory at this school.

  ....

  c Driving along this road is not permitted.

  ....

  d Wearing a uniform is obligatory in this job.

  ....

  e Retiring at 65 is obligatory in some companies.

  ....

  f Going to see a doctor would be a really good idea, I think.

  ....

  g Tell me if you are going to be late. I insist.

  ....

Reading

9 Read the text on the next page and then complete this table. The first answer is done for you.

  a Name:
  Jean–Michel Basquiat

  b Dates (of birth/death):

  c Place of birth:

  d Parents' nationalities:

  e Occupations mentioned (3):

  f Places where exhibitions were held:

  g Name of the film about the main character:

  h Actors in the film:

10 Read through the text again. Note down the names that go with each of these descriptions.

  a He was born in New York. ....

  b It was the place where Basquiat slept in a cardboard box. ....

  c He used the tag 'SAMO'. ....

  d She was Basquiat's girlfriend. ....

  e He was a famous friend of Basquiat. ....

  f He lived for 27 years. ....

  g He was Basquiat's assistant. ....

  h He was an artist who worked with Basquiat. ....

  ....

  i He made a film about Basquiat. ....

An extraordinary life

How a New York graffiti artist became the darling of the art world, but did not live to tell the tale

David Bowie and Jeffrey Wright as Andy Warhol and Jean-Michel Basquiat

Jean-Michel Basquiat
Untitled (Skull), 1981
acrylic and mixed media on canvas
81 x 69 ¼ inches
The Eli and Edythe L. Broad collection
Photograph © Douglas M. Parker Studio
The Broad Art Foundation

Jean-Michel Basquiat, who was born in New York in 1960, was the son of a Haitian father and a Puerto Rican mother. As a child he liked drawing pictures, and because they were good his mother encouraged his interest.

At the age of 18 Basquiat left home and quit school just before he was due to graduate. He had nowhere special to live. Sometimes he would sleep in a cardboard box in Thompkins Square Park. Sometimes he would stay with friends. He played in a band, and started doing graffiti, tagging walls and subway cars with the signature 'SAMO'. But he also painted – a curious mixture of words and images, of western art and the traditions of Haiti, Puerto Rico and Africa. It seemed to many that he was searching for some kind of identity.

Basquiat's paintings were first shown in a joint exhibition in 1980, and immediately people started to get interested – very interested. Soon he was surrounded by agents, gallery owners, journalists and many other people who were desperate to make him famous and make money out of him. His fame spread like wildfire and everyone was talking about him. There were exhibitions of his work all over America. He dated the (not yet famous) pop star Madonna and became a great friend of Andy Warhol, one of the giants of the New York art scene. In 1986 he went to the Ivory Coast in Africa. In 1988 he had simultaneous exhibitions in Paris and New York. But that was the year when it all came to an end. Jean-Michel died of a drug overdose at the age of 27.

Basquiat is still remembered today, not just because he was the first black artist to have real success in the white world of art, but also because he was a fascinating, beautiful man. One writer wrote of him as a 'radiant child'. John Seed, who worked as his assistant when he was at the height of his powers, says that he was 'completely original'. He remembers the first day he met him. Even though he was successful Jean-Michel lived in a room with only two pieces of furniture: a bed and a television. There were books and paintings all over the floor. He remembers too how Basquiat turned up late at his first big exhibition, listening to his personal stereo. He was not comfortable with large crowds, yet many people loved him as one of the most creative and kind people they had ever met.

One fellow artist who knew and worked with Jean-Michel was Julian Schnabel. Nearly ten years after his friend's death he made a film called, simply, *Basquiat*, a celebration of an extraordinary life. It stars Jeffrey Wright as Jean-Michel, David Bowie as Andy Warhol and Courtney Love as a Madonna-like character. There are other roles for well-known actors such as Dennis Hopper.

One scene shows Basquiat behaving as Schnabel wants to remember him. Jean-Michel is in a restaurant with a girlfriend. Suddenly he pours syrup all over the table, spreads it with a paper napkin, and then, with his fork, draws a perfect portrait of the girl sitting opposite him. Then he smiles and he is happy.

11 Look at the way the words and phrases in the box are used in the text on page 61 and then write them in the correct gaps (a–h). You may have to change some of the words.

> at the height of (his) powers
>
> encouraged (his) interest
>
> image
>
> quit school
>
> searching for some kind of identity
>
> simultaneous
>
> star (verb)
>
> syrup

a .... is a thick, sweet liquid.

b .... is another word for a picture, photograph etc.

c If someone doesn't really know who they are but wants to know, they may well be

....

d If someone leaves education before the time they are due to finish, we can say that they

....

e If someone supports you in something you like doing and helps you to do more of it, we can

say they ....

f Two things that happen at the same time are .... happenings.

g When someone is the principal actor in a film. we say the film .... them.

h When someone is doing their best work (and probably being very successful), we can say that

they are ....

Functional language: asking for and giving/refusing permission

12 Put the words of these conversation lines in order. Pay attention to the punctuation and add capital letters where necessary. The first one is done for you.

a A: ? /allowed / are / children / here / in

Are children allowed in here?

B: course / of / , / . / sure

Sure, of course.

b A: take / here / I / if / is / ? / it / photograph/ a / OK

....

B: didn't / I'd / . / rather / you

....

c A: all / bring / dog / here / ? / I / if / in / is / it / my / right

....

B: but / , / keep / . / it / it's / quiet / yes / okay

....

d A: do / I / if / mind / ? / photographs / some / take / you

....

B: afraid / I'm / not / . / possible / that's

....

e A: bring / can / the / ? / friend / I / my / to / party /

....

B: come / she's / sure / . / . / to / welcome

....

f A: can / ? / I / of / one / programmes / take / these

....

B: help / . / . / sure / yourself

Writing: cohesion

13 Rewrite this newspaper article in the box on the right. Make the following changes:

a Make the headline shorter and more dramatic.

b In the main text replace *Mark Sherman*, *Angela Crabtree* and *classical music* with *he*, *him*, *his*, *she*, *her*, *them* or *it* where they are appropriate.

A NOISE WAR HAS BROKEN OUT BETWEEN TWO NEIGHBOURS IN A VERY QUIET RESIDENTIAL AREA

Trouble erupted in a quiet street last night when two neighbours declared a war of noise which involved the police and everyone within a two-mile radius.

The trouble started because Mark Sherman, who is a light sleeper, finally got fed up with Mark Sherman's neighbour's music. Mark Sherman's neighbour, Angela Crabtree, played her electric guitar every night, sometimes until quite late and also threw late-night parties for Angela Crabtree's friends. Every time Angela Crabtree's neighbour complained about the noise, Angela Crabtree either ignored Mark Sherman or told Mark Sherman not to be such a killjoy.

Finally, in desperation, Mark Sherman went and bought a massive sound system which Mark Sherman put in Mark Sherman's garden. Mark Sherman played classical music for two long and noisy nights. At first Mark Sherman's neighbour tried to ignore the classical music, but finally the classical music got too much for Angela Crabtree and Angela Crabtree called the police, but not before the police had received calls from Mark Sherman's and Angela Crabtree's neighbours.

'We have spoken to Mr Sherman and Miss Crabtree,' says Sergeant Maureen Cresswell, 'and we are hoping to encourage Mr Sherman and Miss Crabtree to come to some kind of agreement.'

Pronunciation: word stress

14 Listen to Track 23 and then divide the words in the box into two lists. The first one is done for you.

amazing ◆ certainly ◆ exactly ◆ forbidden ◆ graffiti ◆ occasion ◆ opinion ◆ permission ◆ sensitive ◆ signature

List 1
(stress on the second syllable):

amazing

List 2
(stress on the first syllable):

REFLECTIONS

REFLECTIONS

Thinking about learning and language: making listening easier

One way of making listening easier is to predict what you are going to hear, using your knowledge of the world. If you know what to expect, you are better prepared for what you are going to hear.

15 Listen to the 'beginnings' on Track 24. Write what kind of spoken event (e.g. asking for directions, acting on a stage, etc.) is taking place.

a *a news broadcast*

b ....

c ....

d ....

e ....

f ....

g ....

h ....

16 Decide which of the listening strategies in the table below you would use for each of the situations in Exercise 15. Complete the table with the letters (*a – h*) from Exercise 15.

Listening for gist
I will try and get a 'general understanding' of what I hear the first time I hear it.

Listening for specific detail
I will try and get just the specific, detailed information I want to know and not worry about anything else.

Listening for details
I will try and listen for details in order to understand what to do next.

Test your knowledge

17 Which of the following statements and questions are correct? Put a tick (✓) or a cross (✗) in the brackets.

a According to the police he is a dangerous criminal. [ ]

b Do you mind that I bring my friend along to your party? [ ]

c I don't think people should be allowed use mobile phones on the train. [ ]

d In my opinion people shouldn't spray-paint walls. [ ]

e Is it OK I take a photograph? [ ]

f Driving fast gives me a buzz – I can't help it! [ ]

g You mustn't wear a suit for your interview. It's not necessary. [ ]

h You should to go to bed earlier than you do. [ ]

i You'd better get more sleep if you want to feel more relaxed. [ ]

j Feeding the animals in the zoo is strictly forbidden. [ ]

Rewrite the items you marked with a cross, to make correct sentences.

The phonemic alphabet

18 Consult the table of phonemic symbols on page 123 and then write these words and phrases in ordinary spelling.

a /ˈpriːsɪŋkt/..

b /ˈlɪtə/..

c /ˈkaːrəlaːm/..

d /ˈpɒlɪsɪ/..

e /grəˈfiːtiː/..

f /ˌstrɪktlɪfəˈbɪdən/..

g /ˌhelpjəˈself/..

Check the words by listening to Track 25.

UNIT 9 Body talk

Reading

1 Read this text about going for interviews and answer the questions on the next page.

home | support | contact us | terms and conditions

Let your body do the talking!

How to survive that interview, by Charlene Stewart

You're going for that all-important interview – for a place in a new school or college, or for a new job. You walk into the room and there they are – the interviewers – waiting to see what you are made of.

But did you know that the actual words you speak are less important than the way you look, the way you behave? Remember, they won't just be listening to you, they'll be watching you too, receiving all the messages you send out, consciously or unconsciously. And then they'll decide whether you are the right person for that place or that job.

NERVOUS? Don't be. Relax. Just follow our seven-point plan.

1 Don't cross anything! Keep arms, legs and feet relaxed and uncrossed. People with folded arms look like they're trying to protect themselves from something. They seem to be saying 'I am not confident'. If you're wearing a jacket, undo the buttons and open it up. An open jacket says 'I am an honest, open person. I have nothing to hide'.

2 Lean forward! Don't sit back. It makes you look tired or nervous. Sit forward, project yourself into the space. Show by the way you sit that you are ready and eager, that you want to be part of the scene.

3 Make direct eye contact! Avoid looking away all the time because it makes you look suspicious. Look directly at the people who are asking you questions or who you are talking to. If you lower your head all the time they won't be able to see the enthusiasm in your eyes.

4 Mirror their actions! One of the best ways of gaining people's trust and confidence is to move in the same way as they do. Listen to the speed at which they're talking, and watch the way they sit or move around. Do the same, but do it slowly at first. You don't want them to think you are making fun of them.

5 Go in confidently! A lot depends on how you enter the room. If you walk in nervously with your head and shoulders down, the interviewers won't think much of you from the outset. Go in with your head held high, a slight smile on your lips. When you shake hands with the interviewers don't be too enthusiastic, but make it strong and decisive. Nobody likes a weak handshake.

6 Use your head! When somebody asks you a question don't just say the first thing that comes into your head. Think about your answers. Always say to yourself, 'Why are they asking this question?' because when you know that, you'll probably be able to give an appropriate answer!

7 Think quickly! Studies have shown that people in interviews get most nervous when there is a silence. So be prepared to speak quickly and fluently. But use your head (see above).

Want to know more?
Enrol on one of our confidence courses.
NOW!

2 Circle the ending that is closest to what it says in the text on page 65 for each of the following.

a The way you look and the body language you use are:

   1 ... as important as what you say.

   2 ... more important than what you say.

   3 ... not as important as what you say.

b It is important to:

   1 ... cross your legs.

   2 ... uncross your legs.

   3 ... look open and relaxed.

c In an interview you should:

   1 ... not look at the people asking questions.

   2 ... look directly at the people asking questions.

   3 ... look away when you are answering.

d At the beginning of an interview you should:

   1 ... show that you are confident.

   2 ... behave quietly and modestly.

   3 ... smile a lot.

e When you are asked a question you should:

   1 ... say to the interviewer 'Why are you asking this question?'

   2 ... think carefully but answer quickly.

   3 ... give yourself time to think carefully before answering, even if this involves silence.

3 Read the text again. Are the following statements *True* or *False* ? Write *T* or *F* in the brackets.

a The web page is really an advertisement for a course or courses on how to survive interviews.   [   ]

b Jackets should be kept undone in interviews.   [   ]

c If you sit forward it shows that you are keen to get the job.   [   ]

d Looking at interviewers makes them suspicious.   [   ]

e Try out your interview in the mirror before you go in.   [   ]

f A firm handshake is a good start to an interview.   [   ]

g A quick answer to a question is more important than saying the right thing.   [   ]

h You should try and understand what the interviewers are thinking.   [   ]

i Silence makes people nervous.   [   ]

4 Find words or phrases in the text which mean the opposite of the following.

a interviewee: ....

b consciously: ....

c become nervous or tense: ....

d crossed: ....

e sit back: ....

f unenthusiastic: ....

g raise: ....

h different: ....

i leave (a room): ....

j indecisive: ....

k not the right kind in the situation: ....

l leave (a course): ....

Vocabulary: body language

5 Make ten 'body movement' verbs using any of the letters in the box (but no others). You can use each letter as many times as you want. One is done for you.

> a ◆ c ◆ d ◆ e ◆ f ◆ g ◆ h ◆ i ◆ k ◆
> l ◆ n ◆ o ◆ p ◆ r ◆ s ◆ t ◆ u ◆ v ◆ w

a *clench*

b ....

c ....

d ....

e ....

f ....

g ....

h ....

i ....

j ....

6 Use the verbs from Exercise 5 to complete the following sentences.

a You can .... your arms, but you usually .... your legs.

b Some people .... their teeth when they are angry.

c When people aren't very interested, they sometimes .... their shoulders.

d Sometimes he .... his head to show that he doesn't understand what's happening.

e She looked at the people in the police line-up and .... her finger at one of them.

f Some people bow when they meet, others .... hands.

g He .... his head in agreement.

h She .... her head to show that she didn't agree.

i They .... their arms in great excitement when they saw him arriving at the airport.

Functional language: directing people's actions

7 Look at the pictures and read the conversations. Put the expressions from the box into the correct gaps in the two conversations.

> Anything else ◆ It's difficult to say ◆ easy to say ◆ fold your arms ◆
> folding your arms ◆ shake your fist ◆ shrug your shoulders ◆
> do this scene ◆ what do I do

a

STEVE (THE ACTOR): How do I play this scene?

MR GOLDSTEIN (THE DIRECTOR):

(1) ....

I think you're probably quite angry in this bit.

STEVE: OK. So what do you recommend?

MR GOLDSTEIN: I think you can come in and

(2) .... at Caspar

as you start talking.

STEVE: (3) .... ?

MR GOLDSTEIN: Well you could

(4) .... then, so

that you go on looking angry.

STEVE: Is this what you had in mind?

MR GOLDSTEIN: Yes, that's the type of thing.

b

MARK (THE ACTOR): How do you want me to

(1) .... ?

MS HOWARD (THE DIRECTOR): That's not

(2) ....

I think you're probably a bit bored in this scene.

MARK: OK. So (3) .... ?

MS HOWARD: Well I think you can show boredom by

(4) .... , or crossing your

legs when you sit down.

MARK: Is that all?

MS HOWARD: Well, you could

(5) .... when she talks to you.

MARK: Like this?

MS HOWARD: Yes, that's the kind of thing.

Listen to Track 26 and check your answers.

Listening

8 Listen to the song *No, they can't take that away from me* on Track 27. Tick the correct statement below.

No, they can't take that away from me is a song about:

a ... a love affair that is finished.   [   ]

b ... clothes.   [   ]

c ... dancing.   [   ]

d ... eating.   [   ]

e ... sleeping.   [   ]

9 Write these words in the correct rows.

beams ◆ dreams ◆ hat ◆ key ◆ knife ◆ life ◆ me ◆ tea ◆ that ◆ three

a Words that rhyme with *see*:
b Words that rhyme with *cat*:
c Words that rhyme with *wife*:
d Words that rhyme with *seems*:

10 Listen to Track 27 again. Which pattern does it follow: *a*, *b* or *c*?

Description	Example
Pattern a: None of the words at the end of the lines rhyme with each other (rhyme = e.g. *moon - soon*).	*The sun is golden* *The sky is blue* *It's when you talk* *That I think of love.*
Pattern b: The words at the end of the first and second lines rhyme. The words at the end of the third and fourth lines rhyme.	*The sun is red* *It's what you said* *That makes me love you* *When the sky is blue.*
Pattern c: The words at the end of the first and third lines rhyme. The words at the end of the second and fourth lines rhyme.	*The sun is red* *The sky is blue* *It's what you said* *That makes me love you.*

Your answer: ....

Louis Armstorng & Ella Fitzgerald, two of the great figures of twentieth century jazz

11 Listen to Track 27 again and complete the following lines from the song. Include words from Exercise 9. The first one is done for you.

a The way you wear

your hat ....

b The way you sip

....

c The memory of all

....

d The way your smile

....

e The way you sing

....

f The way you haunt

....

g The way you hold

....

h The way we danced

....

i The way you changed

....

12 Match the phrases in the two columns to make sentences. The first one is done for you.

a It's more expensive if you want a hotel

b I need to buy a car

c They are building a new mosque

d Do you know that song *Lady in*

e I'm waiting for the man

f Did you enjoy *Men*

g David Hockney is one of the most successful painters

h Have you got the latest book

i I really don't like the design

j In Sergio Leone's films there are usually a lot of men

k In Madrid there is a wonderful portrait

1 of the King of Spain.

2 from the vehicle recovery service. My car's broken down.

3 *red*?

4 at the end of my street.

5 on the cover of that book.

6 near the seafront.

7 *in Black*?

8 with beards.

9 with a big engine and a large boot.

10 of his generation.

11 by J.K. Rowling?

13 Complete these descriptions of some family photographs, using either a present or past participle of the verb in brackets in the gap.

a The small boy (lean) .... on the chair next to my grandmother is my father.

b This is the first photo (take) .... by my sister.

c The boy (hold) .... the cat is my cousin James.

d That's my sister sitting on the car (own) .... by my father at the time.

e The lady (sit) .... in the chair is my grandmother.

f This is the pony (give) .... to me by my mother when I was 10.

g This girl (get) .... married is my sister Karen.

14 Write sentences using the phrases in brackets to describe the nouns in blue in each sentence. You may have to add some words, and choose the right form of the verb. The first one is done for you.

a I like pictures of people (interesting faces)

I like pictures of people with interesting faces.

b Steve has three suits (expensive/design (v)/by Armani)

....

c I used to live in a(n) apartment (large/centre of town)

....

d When you are driving in the snow, you have to be careful of cars (skid (v)/on the ice)

....

e In London tourists often take photographs of soldiers (wear/red uniforms/black 'busby' hats)

....

f I've just bought a(n) edition of a book (first/write/Steve McCormack)

....

g The man is the prime suspect in the case (bald/sit in the corner)

....

h My brother really wants to buy a boat like that yacht (small/sail/on the lake)

....

i Frank's going to get tickets for the band (rock/playing/the Zodiac tonight)

....

Writing: written statements

15 There are fourteen spelling mistakes in this witness statement. Can you find them and correct them? The first one is done for you.

Correct spelling

coming

WITNESS STATEMENT FORM

NAME: Mina Parsons
ADDRESS: 26a Victory Mansions, London SE28

STATEMENT
I was walking along the street, ~~cuming~~ from the supermarket. I saw two men run out of the post office. They were waring black hoods with holes for the eys and mouth. One of them was carrying a large bag and they both had what loked like guns in there hands.

They ran in my direcsion and then they ran into the road and stoped a taxi. They forced the driver to get out and then they drove away in his vehicle. Althow I couldn't see the mens faces, I could tell that one of them was quite torl and thin, but the other one – the one houlding the bag – was short and fat. He had trubble running.

I was later told that the men had rubbed the post office and taken a quantity of money from the staff and custermers.

Signed: Mina Parsons   Date: 19 June

Pronunciation: sentence stress

16 Read the following sentences aloud and think about where the stress goes.
Now listen to Track 28 and write the number of the rhythm pattern that matches each sentence. The first one is done for you.

a Are you waving at me? ☐

b Don't raise your eyebrows at me! ☐

c Don't shake your fist at me! ☐

d I am telling the truth. ☐

e I quite agree with you. ☐

f I'm pleased to see you. ☐

g It's so nice to see you. ☐

h Stop biting your nails! 1

REFLECTIONS

Thinking about learning and language: when you can't think of the right word

17 What do you do when you are having a conversation in English and you can't think of a word? Complete the table by ticking the correct boxes.

When I can't think of a word in English I:	often	sometimes	never
...improvise – I come up with any word or phrase that might work, even though I know it isn't the right one. I guess.			
... leave it out – I decide not to try and say what I was going to say and I start talking about something else.			
... 'foreignise' – I try and give an English version of a word in my language in the hope that the person I am talking to will understand what I want to say.			
... paraphrase – I try and explain the idea in a different way by using other words.			
... do something else. (Write what it is.)			

Which do you think is the best option and why?

....

....

....

18 How would you describe the following in conversation (if you didn't know the words for them)?

a ....

b ....

c ....

d ....

e ....

f ....

Test your knowledge

19 Translate the following sentences into your language.

a When I asked him how he felt, he shrugged his shoulders.

b She raised her eyebrows in surprise.

c Look over there. Peter's the one wearing a jacket.

d He listens to music written by Norah Jones.

e He shook his clenched fist at me.

f 'You're absolutely right,' he agreed, nodding his head enthusiastically.

g Are you telling me the truth?

h He's the one with the green jacket and a beard.

i Mother praises children's hospital doctor (*newspaper headline*)

j The food served by our hosts was absolutely delicious.

The phonemic alphabet

20 Consult the table of phonemic symbols on page 123 and then write these words and phrases in ordinary spelling.

a /ˈaɪbraʊ/ ....

b /ˈʃəʊldə/ ....

c /ˈskrætʃɪŋ/ ....

d /ˈwɪtnɪs/ ....

e /ˌtelðəˈtruːθ/ ....

f /ˌtelɪŋðəˈtruːθ/ ....

g /ˌfeɪstəˈfeɪs/ ....

◁))) Listen to Track 29 to check your answers.

Reading

Star check

Karen Chen is a film designer who has worked on films such as 'Beatrice', 'Trials and Efforts' and 'Romance in the Afternoon'. She tells Jane Markon about the gadgets in her life.

Are you a technophobe or a technophile?

I'm definitely a technophile. I love technology because it saves me time and makes me money, so I use it all the time. My husband doesn't agree at all. He's a bit old-fashioned like that. I've only just managed to get him to buy his first mobile phone! But, as for me, I leave home at about 6.30 in the morning, after downloading emails on to my laptop. I deal with all my correspondence on my 55-minute journey to work – it's a good thing we live just near the train station. Then I do the same again – I download new emails before I leave work at about 5.15. It takes me the same time to get home, and by the time I get home I've finished for the day.

Which pieces of technology are important to you?

Three things: my laptop, my mobile phone, and my digital camera. I document everything: the kids, art, buildings, clothes, scenes that catch my eye as I walk past. My digicam has made taking photographs so much easier – and it's easier to send them to people. None of all that messy developing and printing!

What do you use your computer for?

Well, as I said, I send emails all the time. But I do a lot of my design work on screen now and I can send my ideas straight to directors and producers. I do a lot of research on the Internet too – there are some fantastic sites around now. You just type in www.google.com to start a search and you're off.

Who uses the computer at home?

The kids use the computer all the time at home. Of course they mail their friends endlessly – and on top of that they're always texting on their mobile phones! They play computer games when they think I or their father aren't looking! They do some of their homework on the computer too. They don't like doing homework, of course, but there are some really good revision sites on the Internet. I do a lot of my shopping on the net now – 15 minutes for a whole supermarket 'visit'! That feels really good. We book our holidays on the Internet too.

Which ISP do you use?

I have used various ISPs to connect me to my email and the Internet. The one I use at the moment is good because I just pay a monthly fee and there is no extra charge to my phone bill. The design of its site and systems is good – it's not too low-tech and not too high-tech.

Do you think email has changed the way we write?

Oh definitely. We use different language, don't we? And we write so much more quickly. I write things like 'c u at 6'. It's a pity we don't keep emails though. Can you imagine a book of letters between famous people being published in 50 years? I can't. But the good thing about emails is that people often send them instead of ringing you up and so you can decide when to answer them in your own time. It stops you being on demand. People can't just ring up and insist on speaking to you for hours.

What pieces of new technology do you think should be invented?

I want something that allows me to be working in my office and spending leisure time with my husband and children at the same time! I suppose that means a machine that can divide me into two!

1 **Read the article opposite and then tick the statements about Karen Chen that are true.**

a Karen Chen is married. ☐

b She leaves home at half past seven in the morning. ☐

c She travels to work by train. ☐

d She gets home at about ten past seven. ☐

e She is not interested in taking photographs. ☐

f She has written a book. ☐

g Homework is popular in Karen Chen's house. ☐

h Karen uses the Internet for shopping. ☐

i She prefers communicating by email than by phone. ☐

j Everyone in Karen's family loves technology. ☐

2 **Match the initials, words and phrases, most of which come from the text, with their meanings (in the box).**

a 'place' on the Internet that you can visit
a small computer that you can carry with you
digital camera
Internet Service Provider
see you
technically complex
World Wide Web
technically simple
Uniform Resource Locator (the address of a website or web page)

a digicam:..

b high-tech:..

c ISP:..

d laptop:..

e low-tech: ....

f site:..

g c u: ....

h URL: ....

i WWW: ....

3 **Complete the following table with details about Karen.**

a Journey time to and from work:	
b The place where Karen deals with correspondence:	
c The most important pieces of technology for Karen:	1
	2
	3
d What Karen and her family use the computer for:	1
	2
	3
	4
	5
	6
e The advantage of email:	

Grammar: relative clauses (defining)

4 Complete the following sentences with an appropriate relative pronoun from the box. Where more than one pronoun is possible, write both. The first one is done for you.

> that ◆ where ◆ which ◆ who ◆ whose

a I bought the computer ..*that/which*... I saw in a magazine.

b I don't like people .... talk about computers all the time.

c The woman .... Tom is engaged to is a computer programmer.

d I want that new mobile phone .... is smaller than a watch.

e She's the computer criminal .... virus caused millions of dollars of damage to big companies.

f A friend .... wallet was stolen cancelled all his credit cards.

g You can buy contact lenses .... change the colour of your eyes.

h Tansi is the name of the dog .... was hit by a car – and survived.

i Andy is the person .... won first prize in the programming competition and then got an amazing job at Computer Solutions.

j The library is the room .... people can read in peace.

5 Look at this grammar explanation (from 10 A in the Mini-grammar in the Student's Book).

> We can leave out the object pronoun in defining relative clauses:
> *The woman (who) I saw in the supermarket is Paul's sister.*
> *I bought a copy of the book (that) John wrote.*
> But this is not possible with subject pronouns:
> *The man who interviewed me was very polite.* (NOT: ~~The man interviewed me was very polite.~~)

Are the following sentences correct? If they are, put a tick (✓) in the brackets and, if not, a cross (✗). If you think you need to add a pronoun, which pronoun would you add?

a Jason's the man Corinne married. [.....] ....

b He's the man met her at the golf course. [.....] ....

c They're the people invited us to their wedding. [.....] ....

d They're the family we have known for longest. [.....] ....

e He bought her the ring was lost later. [.....] ....

f That's the ring he gave her. [.....] ....

g His mother was the one cried all the time. [.....] ....

h This is a picture of the party went on all night. [.....] ....

6 Match the relative pronouns with the relative clauses and then write them in the correct gaps in the story. The first one is done for you

> which ◆ who ◆ whose ◆ that

> had once been his girlfriend
> he had ever seen
> he thought she would hate
> she had given him all those years ago
> invented this stupid machine
> is electronically sensitive
> meant that nobody had to fill in tickets any more
> served him

Giles was very excited. He had been invited out by someone (**a**) *who had once been his girlfriend* . Giles wanted to wear the jacket (**b**) .... , so he took it to the dry cleaners. When he got there, the sales assistant (**c**) .... explained the computer system. She was especially enthusiastic about the recording system (**d**) .... 'You see,' she said, 'you just give me that jacket, and I put it in this basket (**e**) .... What do you think?' Giles was amazed. It was the most impressive thing (**f**) .... But when he went back to the dry cleaners two days later, the sales assistant couldn't find his jacket even though she searched for it for hours. 'What about the new system?' Giles protested. 'I can't help that,' she said, 'I'm not the person (**g**) ....' There was nothing that Giles could do. He went to the restaurant in an old jacket (**h**) .... When he walked in, his friend introduced him to her new husband.

7 Look at the picture. What does the round-the-world sailor have in her cabin? Write the correct word for each letter.

a ....

b ....

c ....

d ....

e ....

f ....

g ....

h ....

i ....

j ....

8 In these extracts from a new computer manual (which hasn't been printed yet) the editor has crossed out words that have somehow been used incorrectly. Write in the correct words, as in the example.

a
∧ ..*keyboard*.. Practise typing on your ~~website~~ and you will soon notice an increase in your typing speed.

b
∧ .... When you start work, click on the ~~bug~~ that you want to open.

c
∧ .... It is a good idea to save your work onto the ~~printer~~ every fifteen minutes.

d
∧ .... When you receive ~~scanners~~ always check them for viruses.

e
∧ .... If your computer has got a ~~hard disk~~, the best thing is to restart it to see if that clears it up.

f
∧ .... If you want to visit a ~~modem~~, you have to go online.

g
∧ .... If you have a big ~~keyboard~~, you can see more than one document at the same time.

h
∧ .... You can copy a photograph by using ~~an e-mail~~ which takes an image of the photo and puts it on your hard disk.

i
∧ .... When your computer ~~prints~~, you lose everything that hasn't been saved so far.

j
∧ .... When you select 'receive', you will be told how many ~~snailmails~~ there are waiting for you on the server.

Functional language: asking for (technical) help

9 Complete the conversation with one word in each gap.

LAUREN: Software solutions. Lauren speaking. (**a**) .... I help you?

CALLER: Yes please. Well, I hope you can.

LAUREN: What seems to be the (**b**) ....?

CALLER: I don't seem to be able to print out the document I'm working on.

LAUREN: Your printer won't work?

CALLER: No.

LAUREN: Are you (**c**) .... you've switched it on?

CALLER: Of course I'm sure.

LAUREN: I'm sorry, but you (**d**) .... what people are like. Sometimes some people <u>think</u> they've switched it on.

CALLER: OK. OK.

LAUREN: So when you (**e**) .... on the printer icon, what (**f**) ....?

CALLER: Well, nothing happens.

LAUREN: Nothing at all?

CALLER: Well, it just says 'printer cannot be found' all the time, but that's ridiculous.

LAUREN: OK, have you looked (**g**) .... the printer folder?

CALLER: Yes, and it says 'preparing to print' and then I (**h**) .... that 'printer cannot be found' message again.

LAUREN: I see.

CALLER: It's driving me (**i**) .... I've got to finish printing off an essay – or my tutor will kill me.

LAUREN: What about going to the control panel and checking you've selected the right printer. (**j**) .... you done that?

CALLER: Yes, yes of course.

LAUREN: Well then, I can't tell (**k**) ....the problem is from here, really.

CALLER: Please (**l**) .... go away. You can't just leave me alone. You've got to help me.

LAUREN: All right. I tell you what. The best (**m**) .... to do is to switch off everything and (**n**) .... all over again.

CALLER: OK, but will you stay on the line while I do that?

LAUREN: All right, if you hurry.

CALLER: Right, I've (**o**) .... off the computer, and now I'm going to switch off the printer, and ... umm ... oh ... umm ... oh dear. The printer ... you see it wasn't ... oh dear, I think I've been a bit stupid.

LAUREN: Sorry?

CALLER: Listen, you've (**p**) .... very helpful. Honestly. Thanks for everything. Goodbye.

LAUREN: No problem. Goodbye. What was all that about?

Listening

10 Listen to the conversation on Track 30. Tick (✓) the words you hear.

a aeroplanes   [   ]
b antibiotics   [   ]
c aspirin   [   ]
d biology   [   ]
e cars   [   ]
f chemistry   [   ]
g computer   [   ]
h cry   [   ]
i injection   [   ]
j laugh   [   ]
k medicine   [   ]
l physics   [   ]
m ships   [   ]
n shout   [   ]
o space station   [   ]
p university   [   ]
q whisper   [   ]

11 Listen to the Track 30 again. Complete the sentences with *Tom* or *Michelle*. The first one is done for you.

a ....*Tom*............ speaks first.

b ....'s going to study science at university.

c .... does not approve of film studies as a university course.

d .... is going to do more than one subject at university.

e .... is very surprised by what .... says. We know this because .... is asked to repeat a statement/an opinion.

f .... thinks ....'s question is stupid.

g .... uses medicine as a subject to persuade .... of a point of view.

h .... is worried that some medicines don't work any longer.

i .... thinks that science is the cause of many problems.

j .... uses the common cold to attack ....'s point of view.

k ....'s going to do a film studies course.

12 What are Tom's criticisms of the things Michelle talks about? Complete the table.

a	Cars and aeroplanes	1 ....
		2 ....
		3 ....
b	Computers	1 ....
		2 ....
c	Drugs/modern medicines	1 ....
		2 ....

Pronunciation: phrase stress

13 Listen to Track 31 and underline the stressed syllable(s).

a Thank you.
b Thank you.
c Thanks a lot.
d Thank you very much.
e Thank you very much for your help.
f No problem.
g Don't mention it.
h Glad I could help.

Writing: TEXT MSGNG

14 Answer the following text messages in 'ordinary English' (not text message English). Then change your ordinary English into text messages.

a wot r u doing this evening?

....

b do u wnt 2 cum 2 the cinema 2moro?

....

c How ru? ruok?

luv ruth

....

d have u seen ne1 2day?

....

Thinking about learning and language: the writing process

15 When we write an essay or a long letter, we usually go through a number of stages. Put the following stages in order, writing *1 – 6* in the brackets.

a Final draft   [   ]
b First draft   [   ]
c Preparation (planning, making notes etc.)   [   ]
d Reviewing and checking (1)   [   ]
e Reviewing and checking (2)   [   ]
f Second draft   [   ]

16 Look at the things (*a – h* below) that you might do when producing a piece of writing, and put them in the appropriate row in the table.

a check language use (e.g. grammar, vocabulary, linking words)
b check punctuation (and layout)
c check spelling
d check your writing for unnecessary repetition of words and/or information
e decide on the information to go in each paragraph, and the order of the paragraphs
f note down various ideas
g select the best ideas for inclusion
h write a clean copy of the corrected version
i write out a rough version

Preparation
First draft
Reviewing & checking
Second/final draft

Test your knowledge

17 Which of the following statements and questions are correct? Put a tick (✓) or a cross (✗) in the brackets.

a Cure for cancer discovered (*newspaper headline*)   [   ]
b This computer is absolutely terrible. It's just money down the drain.   [   ]
c By the time you finish the exam, you will have been in the exam room for three hours.   [   ]
d He's the person whose house was destroyed by fire.   [   ]
e She's the woman took my photograph yesterday.   [   ]
f People don't use computers find life difficult.   [   ]
g They're the people I met on holiday.   [   ]
h When the computer crashes you have to switch off and start again.   [   ]
i Do you know how connect up to the Internet?   [   ]
j Have you checked connection to the printer?   [   ]

Correct the items you marked with a cross.

The phonemic alphabet

18 Consult the table of phonemic symbols on page 123 and then write these words and phrases in ordinary spelling.

a /ˈkælkjəleɪtə/ ....

b /ˈmɒnɪtə/ ....

c /teləˈvɪʒən/ ....

d /prəˈfɪʃənt/ ....

e /kəmˌpjuːtəˈvaɪrəs/ ....

f /ˌaʊtəvˈdeɪt/ ....

g /kənjuːˈhelpmiː/ ....

Listen to Track 32 to check your answers.

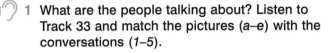
Listening

1 What are the people talking about? Listen to Track 33 and match the pictures (a–e) with the conversations (1–5).

a Conversation ....

d Conversation ....

b Conversation ....

e Conversation ....

c Conversation ....

2 Listen to Track 33 again. Write which conversations (1–5) the following sentences refer to. The first one is done for you.

a One person laughed a lot, the other did not.
Conversation ..4......

b One person really wants to talk about the event. The other is not so keen.
Conversation ....

c One person thought something was frightening. The other person thought it was quite (but not very) frightening.
Conversation ....

d One person thought something was funny but the other is not so sure.
Conversation ....

e Someone doesn't much like art.
Conversation ....

f The speakers want to see something again.
Conversation ....

g The woman and the man disagree about the picture. Conversation ....

h Two people agree that a picture is lovely.
Conversation ....

i Two people really enjoyed being scared.
Conversation ....

3 Complete these extracts from Track 33 with one or more words for each gap.

a Look at that girl .... – the way the sunlight .... her hair.

b It's just so full ....

c She doesn't look like .... at all.
And all those people ...., they're supposed to be musicians, are they?

d Well, perhaps I just ....

e I could .... most of the time.

f I .... laughing.

g But it was ...., wasn't it?

h There's .... a good piece of live theatre.

4 Complete the sentences with the words in the box.

action ◆ animated ◆ autobiography ◆
biography ◆ comedy ◆ comic ◆
detective ◆ historical ◆ horror ◆
musical ◆ opera ◆ romance ◆
romantic comedies ◆ science ◆
thrillers ◆ tragedy ◆ war

a   A .... novel makes you laugh. So does a
.... in the theatre.

b   A book about love and relationships is called a ....
Funny films where boy and girl fall in love in the end are called
....

c   A play which ends in sadness and disaster is a ....

d   A play with singing and music is a ....

e   A show with classical music, an orchestra and singers who do
not use microphones is a called an ....

f   A story, in which a clever person discovers who the murderer is,
is a .... story.

g   Books that are exciting because there is a lot of action in them
are called ....

h   Fiction about the future is called .... fiction.

i   Films about war are called .... films.

j   Films that frighten people are called .... films.

k   Films with a lot of action (fights etc.) are called ....
films.

l   If someone writes a book about their own life, we call it an
.... If they write about someone else's life we
call it a ....

m   Stories about the past are called .... novels.

n   When people draw pictures for a film we call it an
.... film.

5 Match the questions in the box to the answers (a–f), as in the example.

What are the best bits in the film?

What's your favourite Bond film?

What part does Halle Berry play in the film?

What's the story of the film?

Who are the main characters in the film?

Who's in it?

a   '....What's..your..favourite..Bond..film?............................'
'It's *Die Another Day*.'

b   '...'
'For me it was the car chase on the ice and when Bond first sees
Jinx. Fantastic!'

c   '...'
'Pierce Brosnan and Halle Berry.'

d   '...'
'She (Halle Berry) is the character called Jinx.'

e   '...'
'The two main characters in the film are, well, James Bond, of
course, and then a character called Jinx. She's different from a
lot of other Bond girls. She's quite a strong person herself.'

f   '...'
'There's no real story. It's about someone who wants to take over
the world. They always are.'

Reading

6 Read this introduction and then write down the names that go with the descriptions (*a–e*).

All I Want, by Margaret Johnson, tells the story of Alex Faye. Alex works in an art gallery. She started the job three weeks ago.

The gallery is in trouble because it sold paintings by an artist called Ralph Blackman – except that they weren't by Ralph Blackman at all, so everyone is very embarrassed by the mistake.

Alex is crazy about her boss, Brad Courtenay. She thinks she's in love with him. Brad is the owner of the gallery. He has taken her to his house.

a The writer of the book: ....
....

b The central character (who works in an art
  gallery): ....

c He owns the art gallery: ....
....

d He's a painter: ....

e The person Alex is in love with: ....
....

7 Read the extract here from *All I Want*. Match the lines (*a–f*) with the numbers in the text. Note the correct numbers in the brackets.

a Do you like them?   [   ]   d Name three paintings by Van Gogh. [   ]

b It's not a snow scene.   [   ]   e Of course I like them!   [   ]

c Just … just not modern art. [   ]   f Oh, what a fantastic view!   [   ]

'This is the studio,' he says, leading the way into a big square room with very large windows.

'(1) ....' I say, crossing to the window to look out. Outside the skies are still dark, but it hasn't started to rain yet. But even in this poor light the view of File Beacon is wonderful. The room is perfect for an artist.

Brad doesn't seem interested in the view. I can hear him moving things around in the room behind me, and when I turn round I notice several paintings leaning against the wall. They're facing the wrong way, but because of the view from the window, I guess they will be landscapes. I'm so sure about it that when Brad turns two round the right way, I can't help but gasp in surprise.

'What is it?' he asks, frowning at me.
'(2) ....'

For a moment I can't think of anything to say. The paintings aren't landscapes at all. To be honest, I've no idea *what* they are. One of them seems to be completely black except for a small green spot in one corner, and the other seems to be all white. All white. It doesn't even have any spots.

'Yes!' I cry quickly. '(3) .... They're ...' But I have to stop because I can't think of how to continue the sentence. Panicking a little, I start another one. 'Is ... is that one a snow scene?' I ask.

My question is followed by a long silence. It's as quiet as it was in the gallery office. I can hear his breathing again. I realise I've made a big mistake.

'No, Alex,' he says at last, '(4) .... It's not a scene at all. I'm not a landscape painter.'

'Oh,' I say swallowing nervously. 'Sorry. I ... don't know much about modern art.'

'So it would seem.' Brad returns his paintings to their place against the wall as if I'm no longer allowed to see them. 'And yet, if I remember correctly, when you came to the job interview, you told me you knew a lot about art.'

It's true. I did say that. OK, I lied. But you see, as soon as I saw Brad, I knew I had to get the job. I was a desperate girl and I took desperate action.

'I ... well, I do know about art,' I say. 'Well, a bit, anyway. (5) ....'

'OK. Who's your favourite artist?' he demands to know.

By now I'm panicking so much that for the moment the only artist's name I can remember is Ralph Blackman's. Luckily I realise it wouldn't be a good idea to say his name, though, and I think for a little while longer.

'Van Gogh!' I shout at last, and he looks at me doubtfully.

'OK,' he says. '(6) ....'
'Umm ...,' I say, thinking hard.
'Two paintings.'
'Umm ...'
'Come on Alex! *One* painting.'

Suddenly I remember one, and shout out its name excitedly. 'Sunflowers!'

Brad doesn't seem to be impressed. He shakes his head. 'Alex, every person in the world has heard of Sunflowers,' he says.

'Well I haven't got a very good memory for names,' I say weakly. 'That's why I can't think of any more titles.'

8 Look back at the text in Exercise 7 on the previous page. Are the following statements *True* or *False*? Write *T* or *F* in the brackets.

a In the extract 'I' is Alex. [ ]

b It's probably going to rain soon. [ ]

c When she goes into the room, Alex sees the back of some pictures. [ ]

d Alex thinks the paintings will be pictures of the countryside. [ ]

e One painting is white with a green spot. [ ]

f Brad paints pictures of the countryside. [ ]

g Alex likes Brad's pictures. [ ]

h Alex always tells the truth. [ ]

i Alex knows a lot about art. [ ]

j Van Gogh is definitely Alex's favourite artist. [ ]

k 'Sunflowers' was painted by Van Gogh. [ ]

9 Is Brad going to fall in love with Alex, do you think? Write a paragraph explaining your answer.

....

....

....

....

....

....

....

....

....

Grammar: the past (and present) of modals

10 Rewrite the following sentences so that the new sentence means the same as the original. Use the words in blue and the word in brackets. The first one is done for you.

a I am sure you were frightened. (must) *You must have been frightened.*

b I imagine that you didn't enjoy the experience. (can't)...................

....

c It is possible that we have met before. (might)...................

....

d It is not possible that he was in London in 2001. (couldn't)

....

e I am sure that they were married. (must)...................

....

f It is possible that she left her bag on the train. (could)

....

g It is not possible that he took that photograph. (couldn't)

....

h It is possible that they were friends once. (might)...................

....

i I imagine that he didn't mean what he said. (can't) ....

....

j It is possible that she phoned earlier. (could)...................

....

11 Circle the correct modal verb in blue.

TEACHER: Someone took the statue of Shakespeare from this classroom. Who was it?

ANGELA: It (**a**) ought to/must have been the school cleaner, sir.

TEACHER: Why do you say that?

ANGELA: Because it (**b**) couldn't/might have been anyone from this class. We're not like that.

TEACHER: Oh come on Angela, it (**c**) might/didn't need to have been any of you. Did someone take it as a joke?

ALL THE STUDENTS: Sir!

TEACHER: Well really. It (**d**) can't/ought to have been the cleaner. I mean, why would she do such a thing?

ANGELA: OK sir, but if it wasn't the cleaner it (**e**) might/should have been Miss Webster.

TEACHER: Miss Webster? Why? You really (**f**) didn't need to/shouldn't make accusations like that!

ANGELA: Well, because she likes, ummm, sculptures.

TEACHER: Oh don't be ridiculous. It (**g**) couldn't/should have been Miss Webster. She teaches art, for heaven's sake, not literature.

ANGELA: But sir, that's why it (**h**) couldn't/must have been her. She (**i**) had to/should have it for her classes to draw Shakespeare.

SIMON: Sir?

TEACHER: What, Simon?

SIMON: It (**j**) can't/didn't need to have been Miss Webster. She was away sick yesterday and Shakespeare was taken before she …

TEACHER: Yes, Simon? Go on.

SIMON: Nothing, sir.

TEACHER: Nothing, sir? You know something about this, don't you?

SIMON: I (**k**) couldn't/might do, sir.

TEACHER: Well then, was it you? Did you steal Shakespeare?

SIMON: Oh no sir. It (**l**) couldn't/shouldn't have been me.

TEACHER: Why not?

SIMON: Because, well, Shakespeare and me, well, we don't get on! You (**m**) should/can't have known that, sir.

12 Read the article published in a school textbook in the year 2492. Write the verb phrases in the box in the correct gaps. The first one is done for you.

> can imagine ◆ might even have organised ◆
> can learn ◆ must have been ◆
> can't have been popular ◆ must have been put up ◆
> can't have had ◆ must have been taken ◆
> do a lot of it ◆ must have been the centre ◆
> hadn't invented ◆ must have cost ◆
> is erected by robots ◆ it was called

COURSE 2967371: ARCHITECTURE IN THE TWENTY-FIRST CENTURY

The new local government building
(**a**) ...must have cost... a lot of money, and it
(**b**) ....with everyone – new buildings seldom were in those days. You (**c**) ....
the local population talking about it, complaining about this huge modern structure. They
(**d**) .... meetings, and even gone on protest marches. Public protest is not just a modern invention. They used to (**e**) .... , even in the twenty-first century.

But in the end the strange shape was built. It
(**f**) .... a fantastically difficult thing to build because in those far-off days they
(**g**) .... the kind of machinery we have today in the twenty-fifth century. Now we can just touch a button and the building
(**h**) .... , our mechanical friends. But in those days, as far as we can tell, they
(**i**) .... that kind of machine to help them, so the whole thing (**j**) .... by primitive humans.

It's a pity that nothing of that time survives on the banks of what was once a great river. We think
(**k**) .... the River Thames or something like that, and it (**l**) ....
of the life of the city. All we have are these photographs which (**m**) .... when the building was opened. One day, perhaps, we will discover more documents, photographs and artefacts so we
(**n**) .... more about life for primitive man back in the year 2001.

13 Write the number of the appropriate reply (on the right) beside the statements on the left.

a I fell off my bicycle in the middle of the street yesterday, but luckily not in front of a car! [ ]

b Yesterday I had to tell my music teacher that I wasn't going to attend her classes anymore. [ ]

c I left my handbag on the train, but luckily someone gave it to a railway official. [ ]

d I saw a ghost last night! [ ]

e I stayed up all night to finish my homework. [ ]

f I went to a fantastic concert last night. [ ]

g I won a prize for my latest book last week. [ ]

h Our cat died last week. We'd had him for 13 years. [ ]

i Someone took me to see a play in a foreign language that I don't speak. [ ]

j We went walking in the mountains, but nobody had brought a compass and we got completely lost. Luckily a man in a light aeroplane spotted us. [ ]

1 How incredible to get it back. I mean, someone might have stolen it.

2 That can't have been easy. What did she say?

3 That can't have been very interesting.

4 That must have been absolutely wonderful.

5 That must have been frightening.

6 Yes, that was lucky. You might have been killed!

7 Yes, that was lucky. You might have been lost forever.

8 You must have been absolutely devastated. You probably still are.

9 You must be absolutely worn out.

10 You must be really proud of yourself.

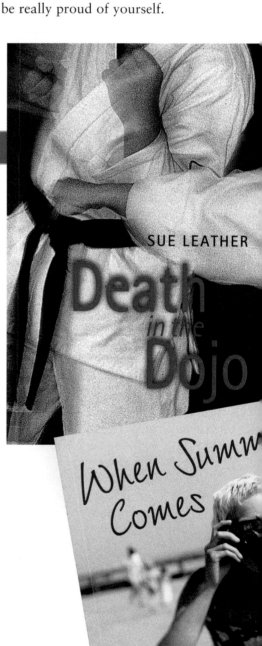

SUE LEATHER

Death in the Dojo

When Summ Comes

14 Look at the book covers and complete the tables for each book.

a What kind of a book do you think it is?

Death in the Dojo
In the Shadow of the Mountain
When Summer Comes

b Write a first line which might be appropriate for a book like this one.

Death in the Dojo
In the Shadow of the Mountain
When Summer Comes

Look at the real first lines from these books on page 86. Were your first lines similar?

Pronunciation: identifying stressed syllables

15 Where is the main stress in each of the following comments? Listen to Track 34 and underline the syllable with the main stress in each sentence.

a You might have hurt yourself.
b You can't have been very pleased.
c That must have been terrifying.
d You could have been in real danger.
e That couldn't have been pleasant.

Listen to Track 34 again and repeat the comments, copying the way they are said.

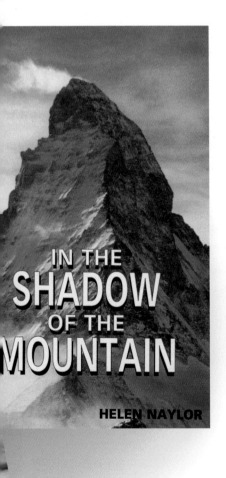

IN THE
SHADOW
OF THE
MOUNTAIN

HELEN NAYLOR

REFLECTIONS

Thinking about learning and language: extensive reading

16 The reading extract in Exercise 7 is from *All I Want*, a novel written especially for students of English. The three books in Exercise 14 are also from similar books. Books like these (often called 'Readers') are designed for 'extensive reading'.

Circle the best answer, in blue, in the following sentences.

a 'Extensive reading' means (1) students reading for pleasure, (2) reading for hours in the classroom and then doing a test, (3) students reading aloud from a book in class.
b Research has shown that one of the best ways of learning English is (1) to read a lot, (2) not to read at all, (3) only to read in class.
c There are (1) a lot of, (2) some, (3) no books specially written for students of English to enjoy reading in English.
d There are readers written for (1) a number of different levels, (2) only two levels, (3) only one level of ability in English.
e If you choose a book at the right level for you, you will find that it is (1) possible and enjoyable, (2) difficult but enjoyable, (3) impossible to read it without a dictionary.

17 Find a Reader which is appropriate for your level – you can ask your teacher for advice or go to a bookshop and see what is there – and read it. Complete these tasks before and after reading it by writing answers to the questions in this table, and the table on the next page.

Before you read the book:

Look at the cover. What is the title?
What do you think the book is about?
Read the titles of the chapters. Now what do you think it is about?
Look at the back of the book for a description. Does it say what it is about?

After you have read the book:

Did you like the book? Why?
How would you describe the book (e.g. *interesting*, *exciting*, *sad*)?
Who was your favourite character?
Who was your least favourite (worst) character?
Write a sentence for other students starting with these words: I think you should/shouldn't read this book because...

Test your knowledge

18 Translate the following sentences and questions into your language.

a Look at the man in the background.

....

b What's that in the top right-hand corner?

....

c Who was that novel written by?

....

d It's based on a novel by Stephen King and it's set in America.

....

e The only thing that matters is your happiness.

....

f He can't have seen the film – it hasn't come out yet.

....

g You might have had an accident!

....

h That must have been terrible for you.

....

The phonemic alphabet

19 Consult the table of phonemic symbols on page 123 and then write these words and phrases in ordinary spelling.

a /aːt/ ....

b /'fɔːgraʊnd/ ....

c /'skʌlptʃə/ ....

d /ɔːtəubaɪ'ɒgrəfɪ/ ....

e /ˌkɒn'trɒvəsiː/ ....

f /'wʌndəfəl/ ....

g /ɪtˌdʌzn'mætə/ ....

Check your answers by listening to Track 35.

First lines (see Exercise 14)

Death in the Dojo: You kill this guy with a karate punch to the left kidney.

In the Shadow of the Mountain: On 23 April 1998, Edward Crowe came out from the glacier on the north side of the Matterhorn mountain above Zermatt in Switzerland.

When Summer Comes: 'When we get to Polreath on Saturday, I'm going to do nothing,' said Anna.

UNIT 12 Not an easy game

Listening

1 Listen to Track 36 and answer the following questions.

a Who is in the sitting room – Geoff or Angela?..............................

b Who is in the kitchen – Geoff or Angela? ....

c Who answers the phone the first time? ....

d Who answers the phone the second time? ....

e Who is the first caller? ....

....

f Who is the second caller? ....

....

g What is Angela's problem?..............

....

h What does Geoff miss? ....

2 Listen to Track 36 again. Are the following statements *True* or *False* ? Write *T* or *F* in the brackets.

a The match is a competition final. [　]

b The game goes into extra time. [　]

c The final score is Liverpool 2, Arsenal 3. [　]

d Geoff's mother has bought a new car. [　]

e Geoff's mother is sympathetic when Geoff says he wants to watch the football, not talk on the telephone. [　]

f Geoff's brother can't persuade a girl to go out with him. [　]

g Geoff's brother is sympathetic when Geoff says he wants to watch the football, not talk on the telephone. [　]

h Angela loves football. [　]

3 In these phone conversations, write what you think the other person is saying based on the words that we hear in Track 36. The first one is done for you.

Conversation 1

GEOFF: Hello? Oh hello (name of caller).

a CALLER: ...What are you doing?........................

GEOFF: Watching the football. Arsenal against Liverpool

b CALLER: ....?

GEOFF: What?

c CALLER: ....?

GEOFF: Yes, it's nearly finished.

d CALLER: ....

GEOFF: Have you? You've seen a new car you want to buy?

e CALLER: ....

GEOFF: Well, I'm sure you can get a different colour if you don't like red. Look Mum, can I ring you back?

f CALLER: ....?

GEOFF: Yes, of course I want to speak to you.

g CALLER: ....

GEOFF: No, no, please don't be upset. I just want to watch the end of this game. You know how important it is.

h CALLER: ....?

GEOFF: Yes, I promise. In about five minutes or so.

Conversation 2

GEOFF: Hello.

a CALLER: ....

GEOFF: Hello (name of caller).

b CALLER: ....

GEOFF: You're feeling unhappy, are you?

c CALLER: ....

GEOFF: Well, if she doesn't want to go out with you I would stop ringing her. But look, can I ring you back? It's the Cup Final.

d CALLER: ....

GEOFF: I know you're my brother.

e CALLER: ....?

GEOFF: Yes, yes, I do care about you. But I'll ring you back.

f CALLER: ....?

GEOFF: Because I don't want to talk right now. Goodbye.

Grammar: conditionals (*if* sentences)

4 Write what the man is saying, using the clauses in the boxes. Start each sentence with the second clause from the sentence before. The first one is done for you.

> 1- go to the shop
> 2- buy a lottery ticket
> 3- watch the lottery programme on TV this evening
> 4- probably be disappointed

a If I need some more milk, _I'll go to the shop._

b If I go to the shop, ...

c ....

d ....

> 5- buy a boat
> 6- sail to the USA
> 7- visit Las Vegas
> 8- lose all my money

e If I win the lottery, ...

f ....

g ....

h ....

5 Match up the two halves of the sentences in the boxes. The first half has a letter and the second has a number.

a If I finish my work before 5,
b Barbara won't be able to go swimming
c If it snows,
d Tom won't be happy
e If Jenny loses her glasses,
f If the taxi arrives soon,
g If Jonathan wants to close a file on his computer,

1 she'll be very upset.
2 he always saves it first.
3 if they don't buy him a cat for his birthday.
4 I'll give you a lift home.
5 Mr and Mrs Thompson will be able to get to the airport in time for their flight.
6 if she forgets her costume.
7 we'll need to put chains on the car wheels.

a .... **e** ....
b .... **f** ....
c .... **g** ....
d ....

6 Read the sentences and then write the correct form of the verb in brackets. The first one is done for you.

a If you ....._were_..... (be) my sister, I .... (give) you my honest opinion but you aren't, so I won't!

b I .... (be) completely amazed if you .... (come) last in the race. But it's not going to happen so I don't need to worry, do I?

c If I .... (be) you, I .... (not/say) that again. That's my advice anyway.

d Before you speak I must just tell you that if you .... (say) that again, I .... (get) really cross. So don't do it, OK?

e It's going to be a tough race, but I have confidence in you. If you .... (win), I .... (be) really happy.

f The light's going. Why are we waiting? If the race .... (not/start) soon, it .... (be) dark.

g We're brothers, but even if you .... (be/not) my brother I .... (still/be) on your side.

h You need a rest. If I .... (be) you, I .... (stop) training for a week.

Reading

7 Read the text that follows and answer these questions. Who:

a ... scored 19 goals? ....

b ... only scored one goal? ....

c ... is the youngest player in Fulham Ladies Football Club? ....

d ... is about to get a doctorate in computer science? ....

e ... has played for the Indian national football team? ....

f ... plays for England? ....

g ... obviously weren't interested in football? ....

h ... thinks it's good that Rachel trains young people? ....

i ... shouted comments that weren't funny? ....

Not just a man's game

Stephanie Merritt meets the young women of Fulham LFC

Photographs by Lina Ahnoff

A damp cold day in February. I watch as two football teams walk off the pitch after a game. The players from the Stowmarket team look exhausted, red-faced, and very very unhappy. Well, you can understand it. They have just lost their game 19-1.

Welcome to the world of women's football! The team that beat Stowmarket is Fulham LFC, the only fully professional women's side in Britain.

Fulham LFC has players of all ages, from 17-year-old Chantelle White to Permi Jhooti, a 30-year-old who has not only played for the Indian national women's team, but is also just finishing her doctorate in computer science. 'If I'm lucky,' she says, 'I'll be able to play for another five years. I do have another occupation, though, and that's what I'll be doing for the rest of my life. But right now I can do what I really love — football — just for a bit longer. I'm really lucky.'

All the players in the team talk about how difficult it was to find female role models in the sport. 'When we were younger it was really hard because there were no women footballers to look up to and admire,' says 21-year-old Rachel Yankey. 'It was definitely seen as a boy's game, and the only well-known players were men. We're trying to change that, to help young girls who want to play football to see that it's not just a man's game.'

That's why, on a cold rainy Monday afternoon, I find myself at a state school in West London. Rachel is training a group of youngsters. They are typical teenagers: the two who are using their mobile phones to send text messages probably won't play for England when they are older, but some of them are really enthusiastic.

'It's really good for girls to be trained by Rachel,' says Clinton Joseph a youth sport coordinator. 'She's a London girl and the kids here see her as a big sister. They know she plays for England, and that sounds pretty good to some of them.'

What do men think of women playing football? 'A lot of the time when you meet blokes and tell them you're a professional footballer they don't believe you,' Chantelle White, 17, explains, 'but when they come and watch us play they're all really surprised at how good we are.' She obviously hasn't encountered the middle-aged man who sat behind me during one match I went to. He was shouting comments that he thought were funny. For example, when the game stopped for injury (something that happens all the time in men's football), he yelled 'What's up ref — does she need to do her hair?' How depressing! This, I thought, was typical male behaviour. But then I looked at the other men around me. They had heard the middle-aged man too but they weren't laughing. None of them thought he was funny at all. Just a sad, old voice from an earlier time.

Women's football isn't a joke any more, even if it ever was. And if you don't believe me, go and watch Chantelle, Rachel, Permi and their team-mates on any Saturday during the season. They're an inspiring sight.

8 Look at the way the following words and phrases are used in the text on page 89, and then write them in the correct gaps (*a–k*) below.

blokes ◆ coordinator ◆ damp ◆ enthusiastic ◆ inspiring ◆ look up to ◆ professional ◆ ref ◆ role model ◆ side ◆ typical

a When the weather is slightly wet, we can say that it is ....

b When someone does a sport for money (rather than just as a hobby) we say they are a ....

c A .... is someone who you try and imitate because you admire them.

d We .... people we admire and respect.

e Someone who is .... is very keen on and involved in something.

f ....is a slang word for 'men'.

g Footballers and football supporters often call the referee '...'.

h Another word for a 'team' in a game is a ....

i Someone who organises different parts of an activity and brings things together is a ....

j Something that is just as you would expect it to be is referred to as ....

k Something that is very good, and makes you want to do better is ....

9 Complete the following sentences about the text.

a We know that Fulham LFC is special because ....

b We know what Permi thinks of football because ....

c We know that players like Rachel had trouble when they started because ....

d We know that some of the students with Rachel weren't interested in football because ....

e We know other men didn't think the middle-aged man was funny because ....

10 Unscramble the letters to make words and then match them with the numbers. The first one is done for you.

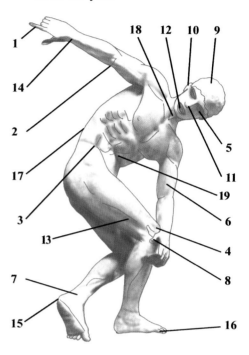

a (a e k l n) *ankle – 7*

b (a m r) ....

c (a b c k) ....

d (a e r) ....

e (b e l o w) ....

f (e e y) ....

g (a d e h) ....

h (e e h l) ....

i (d e i n x e f g i n r) ....

j (e e k n) ....

k (e g l) ....

l (e i l l t t o e t) ....

m (e n o s) ....

n (a h o r t t) ....

o (b h m u t) ....

p (h o o t t) ....

q (a i s t w) ....

r (i r s t w) ....

s (m a t h c o s) ....

11 Look at the pictures. What's the person's problem? Use words from Exercise 10. The first one is done for you.

a She's got a stomach-ache.

b ....
....
....

c ....
....
....

d ....
....
....

e ....
....
....

f ....
....
....

12 Write one word in each gap. The first one is done for you.

TRACEY: Hi Marlene, (a) ....how........ are you?

MARLENE: Oh fine. Well I am now. It's

(b) .... to be back.

TRACEY: Yes, I agree. Holidays back at home with your family are pretty stressful.

MARLENE: It's not so much that. I mean my family are pretty wild, it's true, but this time it (c) .... really their fault.

TRACEY: Why? What was the (d) .... ?

MARLENE: I got ill. Caught flu or something, so I was in

(e) .... for about a week.

TRACEY: Oh, I'm (f) .... to hear that. But you're better now.

MARLENE: Yes, more or less. But it didn't help that my father had just

(g) .... his leg.

TRACEY: How did he do that?

MARLENE: He fell when he was (h) .... football with my little brother.

TRACEY: Is his leg in plaster now?

MARLENE: Yes, and he complains all the time. Honestly!

TRACEY: Typical man.

MARLENE: Yes. Anyway, what (i) .... you? How are you, I mean really.

TRACEY: Oh, I'm fine. I wasn't feeling very (j) .... either for a couple of days, but now that I'm back here I feel absolutely great.

MARLENE: Great. So tonight

(k) .... go to the beginning-of-term party at the Students' Union!

TRACEY: Brilliant idea!

13 You work on a newspaper 'problem' page. People write to you about their problems and you give them advice on what to do.

Read the problems, below, and then say which problem the following advice statements (a – i) are designed to answer. The first one is done for you.

a Buy another television. ....Problem 1........

b Tell them that you're not big but you can run fast. ....

c Find a club outside school where you can play (and where you'll get picked more often). ....

d Get bigger. ....

e Go on a sun, sea and sand holiday instead. ....

f Go out every time there's a match on. ....

g Go to the gym and get stronger. ....

h Take up another sport which isn't so dangerous. ....

i Tell him, 'it's either football or me!' ....

Problem 1

Dear Problem Page,
My husband is football crazy. He talks about it all the time, and watches every football match on television, so I can never watch what I want to watch. What can I do?
Yours,
Jane (a football widow)

Dear Problem Page,
I love skiing. It's my favourite sport. But every time I go on a skiing holiday, I break something – my leg, a wrist, my collar bone. What can I do?

Yours,

Tom

Problem 2

Problem 3

Dear Problem Page,

I am at secondary school and I love playing rugby, but the problem is when they pick teams I am always the last to be picked. I'm quite small for my age, and I want them to choose me first. What can I do?
Waiting to hear from you,
Rugby loser

14 Now write your advice for any two of the problems using one piece of advice from the previous exercise for each problem, as in the example.

In answer to problem [1]:

Dear Jane,
Your problem sounds very serious. But I think there is a way of resolving it. If I were you, I'd buy another television – then you can watch what you want when you want.

15 Listen to Track 37. Tick (✓) the words or phrases you hear.

a shoulder [ ]
  soldier [ ]
b toys [ ]
  toes [ ]
c I'd give him a ring [ ]
  I'd give it to him [ ]
d If you ran home [ ]
  If you rang home [ ]
e free tickets [ ]
  three tickets [ ]

Listen to Track 37 again and repeat what the speakers say.

REFLECTIONS

Thinking about language and learning: notebooks

16 Which of the following notebook entries do you prefer and why? Complete the sentence at the end.

Vocabulary notebook entry 1
(the words or phrases are written in alphabetical order)

ankle

elbow

goalkeeper

manager

referee

shoulder

Vocabulary notebook entry 2
(the words are written in alphabetical order and include a translation into the student's own language)

ankle	tobillo
elbow	codo
goalkeeper	portero
manager	gerente/entrenador
referee	árbitro
shoulder	hombro

Vocabulary notebook entry 3
(the words or phrases are in alphabetical order, with or without a translation, and with an example sentence)

ankle	I sprained my ankle when I was running.
elbow	I hit my elbow on a shelf and it hurts!
goalkeeper	The goalkeeper couldn't stop the ball going into the net.
manager	The manager told the players that they were all sacked.
referee	The referee blew his whistle to start the game.
shoulder	After a few hours at the computer my neck and shoulders ache.

Vocabulary notebook entry 4
(words that are connected are written together)

People in football:	goalkeeper
	manager
	referee
Parts of the body:	ankle
	elbow
	shoulder

Vocabulary notebook entry 5
(some other system – explain what it is: ....

....

......................................)

I prefer notebook entry number ...... because ....

....

....

....

....

....

When you have finished, look at the notes on page 94.

17 What words and phrases from Unit 12 in the Student's Book and the Workbook (and which aren't in the lists on page 128 in the Students' Book) are you going to write in your vocabulary notebook?

unit twelve 93

18 Which of the following statements and questions are correct? Put a tick (✓) or a cross (✗) in the brackets.

a If the referee gives you a red card, you had to leave the pitch. [ ]

b The defenders couldn't stop the ball from going into the net. [ ]

c If I am you, I wouldn't do that! [ ]

d I've had enough of you reading my thoughts all the time! [ ]

e If you've got a ticket, go through the green door. [ ]

f I'm not rich, but if I was I'll buy a new car. [ ]

g I've got a tooth hurt. It's really painful. [ ]

h You're looking well. [ ]

i I'm not very well. I'm feeling a bit on the weather. [ ]

j She's got bad food poisoning. [ ]

Rewrite the items you marked with a cross, to make correct sentences.

19 Consult the table of phonemic symbols on page 123 and then write these words and phrases in ordinary spelling.

a /dəˈfendə/ ....

b /ˈɪndʒəriː/ ....

c /refəˈriː/ ....

d /ˌbrəʊkənˈtəʊ/ ....

e /ˈstʌməkeɪk/ ....

f /ˈtreɪnɪŋseʃən/ ....

g /ˌʌndəðəˈweðə/ ....

Check your answers by listening to Track 38.

Notes (for Exercise 16):

• Listing words alphabetically (entry 1) can be helpful but some people prefer more information about meaning and use.

• Translating words (entry 2) can help you check meaning very quickly, but translaton is not always easy.

• It's often a good idea to write in example sentences (entry 3) to remind you of how the word is used.

• Organising words into meaning groups (entry 4) often helps people remember words more effectively.

UNIT 13 More than music

Reading

1 Read the following statements. Do you agree with the statements? Put *A* (= *Agree*), *D* (= *Disagree*) or *DK* (= *Don't Know*) in Column 1.

		Column 1	Column 2
a	A lot of music sounds the same.		
b	It is good fun to play a musical instrument.		
c	It is very important to listen to music as often as possible.		
d	Music can be enjoyed equally by people who are musicians and those who don't 'know' anything about it.		
e	Music is important for special occasions.		
f	People from all cultures react to music.		
g	The best reason for music is so that you have something to dance to at a club or party.		
h	Too much music is played through loudspeakers in public places.		
i	Writing music on a computer is easy.		

Now read the newspaper article on this and the next page. Write the names of the people who have the opinions (*a–i*) in column 2 above.

HOW IMPORTANT IS MUSIC?

On National music day we sent our reporters out to ask people on the streets what they thought about music. Here's what they said.

Music? I hate the stuff. You have to listen to it in shops, supermarkets, town centres, airports, everywhere! There's always music playing in the background. And you know what I hate most? When you ring up some company and they put you on hold and play you some classical music. The Four Seasons! Vivaldi! Give me a world without music, and the sooner the better.

Colin Parker, 47, taxi driver

I can't live without music. I listen to it all day when I'm working. Music of all kinds. It's always on in the background. It helps to keep me happy! It stops me getting bored. If you deprived me of music for a day, I'd be completely miserable!.

Marina Volskov, 32, writer

Yeah, music's cool. Not classical stuff, or pop music or something like that. It's got to have a beat, got to be good to dance to. The point of music is to make you feel happy, make you want to have a good time with your friends. I'm working on some stuff on my computer at the moment. You just select a beat and some sounds, and the software creates a whole track for you. It's magic.

Ricki Bartram 23, student

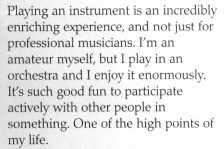

Playing an instrument is an incredibly enriching experience, and not just for professional musicians. I'm an amateur myself, but I play in an orchestra and I enjoy it enormously. It's such good fun to participate actively with other people in something. One of the high points of my life.

Pauline Johnson, 52, housewife

It's an enigma, isn't it? I mean almost everyone listens to music of some kind, and everyone understands it. You don't have to be a musical expert to know when a piece of music is sad or when it's happy. Everyone can recognise a piece of warlike music or something very warm and romantic. It doesn't even seem to matter what culture you come from. Everyone responds to music in some way or other. Even more than the visual arts, I think. But then I would say that. I teach music at a local school!

Tony Collins, 29, teacher

I don't really think about music much. It doesn't interest me. I think I'm more of a visual person. Some people seem to have an ear for music. The moment they hear a tune they can recognise it, but most of it sounds the same to me. I do like a bit of music at important moments, though, like a wedding or something. But that's about it.

Sally James, 19, secretary

2 Who:

a ... always has music playing wherever he or she is? ....

b ... can't recognise different pieces of music?
....

c ... doesn't pay much attention to music?
....

d ... enjoys working with other people?
....

e ... has computer programs that 'write' music?
....

f ... hates recorded music on telephones?
....

g ... needs music to be happy?
....

h ... thinks music is more important than pictures?
....

i ... thinks rhythm is the most important aspect of music? ....

j ... understands pictures better than music?
....

3 Look at the way the words and phrases in the box are used in the text on page 95 and on this page, and write them in the correct gaps below.

deprived ◆ enigma ◆ enriching ◆
have an ear for ◆ miserable ◆ participate actively ◆
put you on hold ◆ visual

a If people understand music and like it (and can sing or play it), we often say they .... music.

b If someone is .... of something, it means they have been stopped from having it, even if they need it.

c If someone is very, very sad, we can say that they are ....

d If something makes our life better, or more colourful or warmer ,we can say that it is ....

e If something or someone is difficult to understand, we can say that it (or he or she) is an ....

f If someone appreciates looking at pictures and designs, we can say that they are a .... person.

g When a telephone operator (or recorded message) asks you to wait for a minute, they ....

h When you join in with something, and you do it enthusiastically, you .... in it.

4 How many different occupations can you find in the word chain? Put a line between
   each word. The first one is done for you.

actor|athletecellistcomposerconductordrummerfootballerguitaristmanagerpercussionistphotographerpianist

receptionistsaxophonistscientistsingertelephonisttherapisttrombonisttrumpeterviolinist

5 What are their occupations?
   Write one of the words from
   Exercise 4 beside each sentence.

a I sit down to do this.
I use a bow and my
instrument has
four strings.

b When I answer,
I have to sound friendly
and polite even when
I'm feeling terrible.

c Sometimes, when
I'm working on a new
piece, I stay up all night
thinking up new
ideas.

d Without people like me
no one would make any
new discoveries.

e There are more people
like me than any others
in a big orchestra.

f I have to train every
morning – usually a four-
mile run. It's exhausting.

g I hate weddings
most of all – trying to get
everyone to stand still and
smile at the same time.

h The best thing is that I
make a lot of different
noises.

i People say we're paid
too much, but if your
team wins, well, why
not?

j I can make people
happy when they
are depressed.

Grammar: verb patterns

6 Circle the correct alternative, in blue, in the following sentences. The first one is done for you

a My brother wanted (to go)/going to the cinema with me.

b He suggested to go/going later that evening and I agreed.

c In the afternoon I decided to go/going to see my friend.

d I promised to get/getting home in time.

e I enjoyed to see/seeing my friend.

f We decided to play/playing tennis.

g We both managed to win/winning some games.

h We finished to play/playing quite late, just as it was getting dark.

i On the way home I avoided going/to go on the motorway.

j I forgot turning/to turn right at the traffic lights and I got completely lost.

k When the police stopped me, I denied to go/going too fast.

l I admitted being/to be lost.

m I dislike to be/being lost.

n In the end the police agreed letting/to let me go.

o I got home far too late, but I offered to go/going to the cinema with my brother on a different evening.

7 Rewrite the sentences using the words in brackets. The first one is done for you.

a I play tennis. (enjoy)

   I enjoy playing tennis.

b I'll finish the job in a couple of hours. (expect)

c Phil said : 'I didn't borrow her bicycle.' (deny)

d Phil said: 'I'll mend it.' (offer)

e Phil: 'I'll buy a new bell.' (agree)

f I didn't do any work yesterday. (avoid)

g I played tennis with my cousin when I was young. (remember)

h I am going to Italy this summer. (want)

i Phil: 'Buy a new computer.' (suggest)

j Me: 'I'll do it.' (decide)

k My cousin didn't come to play tennis with me. (forget)

8 Make sentences by matching words from columns *A* and *B*. Each phrase can only be used once. The first one is done for you.

Column A	Column B	
a Jack admitted	1 playing football by pretending he was ill.	a ....2....
b He denied	2 being in Bob's room.	b ....
c Jack managed to avoid	3 to go home yet.	c ....
d I didn't see you yesterday. At least I don't remember	4 playing the cello when I left school.	d ....
e I don't like sport and I hate	5 seeing you.	e ....
f I know I've lied in the past but this time I promise	6 taking Bob's money.	f ....
g Would you like	7 to tell you the truth.	g ....
h I still like singing but I stopped	8 to take his drumsticks to the rehearsal.	h ....
i I know it's late but I don't want	9 to share my pizza?	i ....
j My shoe felt loose so I stopped	10 watching it.	j ....
k The drummer forgot	11 to tie my shoelace.	k ....

9 Listen to Track 39 and draw a line connecting the speakers to the instruments they play (not all the instruments are played by them).

Carol

Daniel

Carmen

Vince

electric guitar

cello

guitar

drums

trumpet

saxophone

10 Listen to Track 39 again.

Who:

a ... didn't mind practising? ....

b ... has to keep practising? ....

c ... had a really good time with music in the past?

....

d ... thinks playing their instrument is good for them?

....

e ... received a good musical start from one of their parents?

....

f ... dreams of a career in music? ....

g ... once dreamed of a career in music which didn't happen?

....

h ... isn't always popular with the neighbours?

....

i ... spends a lot of their leisure time playing music?

....

j ... doesn't spend any time playing music?

....

11 Complete the following extracts from Track 39.

a I .... for quite a few years.

b I've still got .... I made in those orchestras.

c Well, there .... and there are so many other things to do.

d She says he spends .... than on his job.

e When I was little .... learning the sax, too.

f I'd like to be a professional musician .... up.

g The whole street .... if I'm not careful.

h Sometimes I just ....

i You .... you're a drummer.

j My mother .... guitar.

k ... and .... to pay for my holidays.

l In the end I couldn't find anyone .... I thought I was.

Functional language: showing concern

12 Put the following lines in the correct places in the conversations below.

1 I don't think I've got the part.
2 I'm really pleased to hear it.
3 I'm sure it wasn't as bad as you think it was.
4 You might have done. There aren't that many good musicians around.
5 It could have been worse.
6 I'm sure I didn't get in.
7 So you think you might have passed?
8 It went brilliantly!

MARK: How was the audition?

JESSY: It was absolutely terrible.

(**a**) ....

MARK: (**b**) ....

RACHEL: How was the interview?

SARAH : (**c**) ....
I think I got the job.

RACHEL: (**d**) ....

CAROL: How was the exam?

JIM: (**e**) ....

CAROL: (**f**) ....

PETER: How was the audition?

JAMES: Horrible. (**g**) ....
They're going to let me know.

PETER: (**h**) ....

Writing: for & against

13 Look at the following statement.

All children should learn a musical instrument at school.

Do you agree with it?

14 Read the following opinions. What do you think?
Write *A* (= *Agree*) or *D* (= *Disagree*) in the brackets.

a Music can be enjoyed all your life. [ ]

b Children take pride in progress. [ ]

c Children develop intellectually if they learn an instrument. [ ]

d Instruments are expensive to buy or hire. [ ]

e Not everyone likes music. [ ]

f There's nothing special about music. [ ]

g Other subjects (e.g. maths, science) are more important. [ ]

h Playing in music groups is good for cooperation. [ ]

i Practising a musical instrument is good for self-discipline. [ ]

j Instrumental playing helps mind and body coordination. [ ]

k Some children are bored by music. [ ]

l Some children have no musical talent. [ ]

100 unit thirteen

15 Now list the opinions (*a–l*) from Exercise 14 in the correct columns below.

For (in favour of) learning a musical instrument	Against learning a music instrument

Use some of the opinions from Exercise 14 to write one paragraph of not more than four sentences, either in favour of or against the statement in Exercise 13.

....

....

....

....

....

....

....

Pronunciation: phrase & sentence stress

16 Read the following phrases and sentences, and say them to yourself. Think carefully where the stress goes. Then listen to Track 40 and number the phrases and sentences in the order of the stress and intonation patterns you hear. The first one is done for you.

a Absolutely terrible.

b I couldn't think what to write.

c I made a real mess of it.

d I think it went OK.

e I'm sure it wasn't as bad as you think.

f It can't have been that bad.

g It could have been worse.

h Oh good!

i Oh you poor thing.   **1**

j That sounds terrible.

REFLECTIONS

Thinking about learning and language: understanding corrections

17 Read the following corrected piece of homework by an elementary student, and then complete the 'correction symbols' table with the correct symbols.

> Music is my faverite [sp] thing. I like very much it [wo]. I
> have learned [t] the piano when I was young but
> now I don't [to] play very much at all.
>   My sister play [c] in a rock band. She is very
> keen/ heavy metal music, though I don't like it
> at all because I am better in [ww] jazz-style music.
>   My friend peter [p] like [c] heavy metal music too.
> He has a lot of informations [g] about it – and he
> also likes a lot my sister [wo]!

CORRECTION SYMBOLS

Symbol	Meaning
a	Something has been left out.
b	Something that is not necessary has been put in.
c	There is a spelling mistake.
d	The student has used the wrong word(s).
e	There is a grammar mistake.
f	The verb doesn't agree with its subject – 'concord'.
g	There is a punctuation mistake.
h	The verb tense is wrong.
i	The word order is wrong.

18 Write a correct version of the student's composition in Exercise 17.

....
....
....
....
....

Test your knowledge

19 Translate the following.

a I have decided to do something about it.

....

b When he agreed to sell her the house she went absolutely crazy! ....

c She stopped talking to her husband. ....

d She stopped to talk to her husband. ....

e What on earth do you think you are doing? ....

....

f When she finally arrived, I breathed a huge sigh of relief.

....

g I made a real mess of my test. I couldn't answer two of the questions. ....

h I'm sure you didn't do as badly as you think you did.

....

The phonemic alphabet

20 Consult the table of phonemic symbols on page 123 and then write these words and phrases in ordinary spelling.

a /'tʃelɪst/......................

b /en'dʒɔɪ/......................

c /sə'dʒest/......................

d /fə'tɔgrəfə/......................

e /ə'kʌmpənɪst/......................

f /ˌaɪm'autəvhjɪə/......................

g /aɪmeɪjəzwəlgəʊ'həʊm/

....

🔊 **Check your answers by listening to Track 41.**

Listening

1 Look at the pictures. What is happening in each one?

Listen to Track 42 and put the pictures in the right order.

1 .... 2 .... 3 ....
4 .... 5 .... 6 ....

2 Answer the following questions.

a Why did the press (newspaper and television news people) come to the narrator's house?

....

b What job had the narrator just left before the story started?

....

c How did the press people get into the garden?

....

d Where did Clem Mullen work? ....

e How well did the narrator know Clem Mullen?

....

f How long did the media interest in the narrator last?

....

g What happened to Clem Mullen? ....

h What did the neighbours think of the narrator?

....

3 Look up the meaning of the following words and expressions in a dictionary and then use them to complete the gaps in the extracts from Track 42.

> find out ◆ hammering ◆ innocence ◆ into thin air ◆ mixed me up ◆
> mutter darkly ◆ on top of ◆ ringside ◆ screeched ◆ secret service

a They had a .... seat.

b The vehicles .... to a halt.

c I heard them .... on my door.

d One of them had fallen .... the dustbins.

e No one liked words like that in the ....

f They must have .... with someone else.

g Some people never really believed in my ....

h He had just disappeared ....

i You soon .... who your real friends are.

j 'No smoke without fire', they ....

4 *'And I think - what would they say if I told them the truth?'* What is the truth, do you think?

Grammar: direct and indirect speech

5 Rewrite the following things that people said in the past as indirect speech. The first one is done for you.

a I've lived here for two years. (Mary)

Mary said that she had lived there for two years.

b I study music. (Peter)

c We work in a software company. (Paul and Kenny)

d I will finish my course in six months. (Mrs Yamanachi)

e I will graduate next year. (Ellen)

f I'm going to join a rock band. (Matt)

g My brother's going to work in a law firm in London. (Sally)

h We've just watched a football match on TV. (Kate and Jane)

i I've just been to New York for the first time. (Simon)

j Can you give me a ring tomorrow? (Anita – to a friend)

k I'll be there in a minute! (Henry)

6 Write down what Marianne (the dancer) is telling her friend about her phone call with Bob. The first one is done for you.

a MARIANNE: Are you coming round tonight?
b BOB: No. I'm going to meet my mates at the skateboard park.
c MARIANNE: Do you want to come round here later?
d BOB: No, thanks. I think it'll be too late.
e MARIANNE: Do you want to come to the ballet with me next week?
f BOB: I don't think I want to see you again.
g MARIANNE: Why? Am I too boring?
h BOB: No, of course not. It's just that I prefer girls who like skateboarding better than ballet.

a I asked Bob if he was coming round that night.

b

c

d

e

f

g

h

7 Read the text. Then write Ruth and Martin's conversation, highlighted, in blue, in direct speech. The first one is done for you.

This is the story of how I met Ruth and what happened afterwards.

One evening I decided to go to the cinema. I bought a ticket and sat down - you could sit where you wanted. A young woman came up to me where I was sitting. (**a**) She asked me if anyone was sitting in the seat next to me, and (**b**) I said that as far as I knew nobody was. So (**c**) she said thank you and sat down and the film started. Well, after about fifteen minutes I couldn't help noticing that she was crying, very quietly. (**d**) I asked her if she was all right, and (**e**) she said that she was, so (**f**) I asked her why she was crying if she was all right – I'm like that, you see, a bit rude! Anyway, (**g**) she told me that the main actor in the film reminded her of her last boyfriend. (**h**) She said he'd left her a year ago. So (**i**) I said that I couldn't understand why anyone would leave her (well because I'm like that) and that made her smile, I'm pleased to say.

By this time (**j**) people around us were asking us to be quiet. This girl blushed at that and so (**k**) I said we had better leave the cinema (the film wasn't that great anyway); so we did. We went to a café. (**l**) I asked her what her name was and (**m**) she said it was Ruth. (**n**) I told her my name was Martin. (**o**) She asked me what I did and (**p**) I told her I was an English teacher. (**q**) She asked if that was interesting and (**r**) I said of course it was.

(**s**) Ruth told me she was a computer programmer and (**t**) that she worked for a big company. (**u**) I said that must be interesting. (**v**) She said that it wasn't, and that she was really bored. (**w**) So I said why didn't she train to be an English teacher and (**x**) she said she'd think about it.

That was two years ago. She's a teacher now. We work in the same language school. We are really good friends and she's just got engaged to one of the other teachers there, so I feel I played an important part in her future happiness!

a Is anyone sitting in that seat?

b ....

c ....

d ....

e ....

f ....

g ....

h ....

i ....

j ....

k ....

l ....

m ....

n ....

o ....

p ....

q ....

r ....

s ....

t ....

u ....

v ....

w ....

x ....

a colleague

b ....

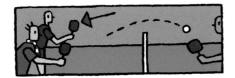

c ....

d ....

e ....

f ....

g ....

h ....

8 Make eight words to describe the relationship of the people in the pictures to Fred, using any of the letters in the box (but no others). Some of the words are singular, some are plural. You can use each letter as many times as you want. One is done for you.

> a c d e g i l m n o p q u r s t y

9 Rewrite the sentences using the words in brackets (exactly as they are written). The new sentences should mean the same as the old ones. The first one is done for you.

a I work in the same office as Mr Perry but we aren't friends or anything. (colleagues)

Mr Perry and I are colleagues.

b My brother and I are not especially good friends. (close to)

I ....

c My grandmother means a lot to me; I like her a lot. (fond of)

I ....

d I admire my cousin. (think a lot)

I ....

e She's in love with Rafael. (crazy)

She ....

f John and I have an easy relationship. (get along well)

John and ....

g Mary and I are not friends. (get on with)

Mary and ....

h I have always admired my uncle. (respect)

I ....

Functional language: inviting someone

10 Put the words in order to make invitations. Write them in the correct places in the conversation by matching them with the answers. The first one is done for you.

1 come / like / sailing / ? / to / Would / you
2 a / coming / Do / fancy / for / meal / ? / out / you
3 a / about / DJ / going / good / How / ? / . / Q club / the / there / There's / to
4 and / come / I / if / like / me / new / play / see / the / to/ . / was / with / wondering / would / you
5 be / birthday / coming / in / interested / my / party/ ? / to / twenty-first / Would / you
6 cinema / come / like / the / to / to/ ? / Would / you

a ' *Would you like to come sailing?* '
'I'd rather not, if you don't mind. I don't like being on water. I can't swim.'

b ' .... '
'Well that depends on what's on.'

c ' .... '
'Yes I'd love to, but I'm a vegetarian, you know.'

d ' .... '
'I'm not sure if I can, but I'd really like to. I love the theatre.'

e ' .... '
'I can't, I'm afraid. I'm going to be away. But I hope you have a great celebration.'

f ' .... '
'I'd rather not. It's always so noisy in there.'

Reading

11 Read the following statements. Tick (✓) the first column if you agree with them.

a Being attracted to someone isn't the same as being in love with them.		
b It's difficult to say whether 'this is love'.		1
c Some people think they are in love, but actually they just don't want to be alone.		
d There are many different kinds of love.		
e When you love someone, you feel as if they are with you even when you are apart.		
f When you love someone, you want to be with them.		
g When you love someone, you want to share everything with them.		
h You can't love someone unless you love yourself.		
i You know whether or not you are in love.		

12 Now read the text on the next page. In what order do the points occur in the text? Write in the numbers in the second column above. The first one has been done for you.

Is This Love? A Closer Look
by Bob Narindra

One of the most common questions we get asked at Lovingyou.com is 'How do you know if it is really love?' Well, as you can imagine, this also happens to be one of the most difficult questions to answer! Love is such a strange, wonderful thing that nobody really understands what it is yet. Another problem is that there are so many different kinds of love: the love you feel for a friend, a family member, a sport or even a pet. Love is such a crazy emotion that there is absolutely no way that I can definitively answer how you know when it is love … but I am going to give it a try!

Now, in order to find out if you love someone, the basic place to start would be to ask yourself, do you want to be with them. If the answer to that question is no, then it really can't be love. When you love someone, you want to be with them. Not just be with them, but share everything with them. You have a great day at work and want to rush home and tell them every wonderful thing that has happened. You feel excited at the prospect of just being in their company; just being close to them isn't enough, you want to be a part of them, a part of their life forever. You can't stand the thought of being away from them but, when you are, you still feel that bond that ties you together wherever you go. You can almost feel what they are feeling. You feel like, with a little bit of effort, you can see what they are seeing and think what they are thinking. That, to me, is love.

Now, on the other side of the spectrum, there are lots of emotions that people confuse with love. One of the most common is attraction. There is a difference between being attracted to someone and wanting to spend the rest of your life with someone.

Some people fall into the trap of thinking they love someone just because they are afraid to be alone. They have become dependent on the other person for so much that they don't know how to make it on their own, or because they would much rather be with someone than no one.

This leads to the old cliché that in order to love another person, you must first learn to love yourself. Well, we've all heard that before, but what does it really mean? It means that you have to be confident in your own ability and your own judgement. You really have to like yourself and know what you have to offer another person. There is no way that you can love another person if you are so neurotic that you do anything they ask and agree with everything they say – just in case they won't like you any more if you don't behave like that.

Basically, the question of whether or not you are in love with someone is pretty obvious: you either are or you aren't … and, deep down, you know the answer. You just have to trust yourself to recognise it.

13 Look at the way the words and phrases in the box are used in the text on the left, and then write them in the correct gaps below.

cliché ♦ complicate ♦ dependent on ♦ fall into the trap ♦ pretty obvious ♦ harmony ♦ judgement ♦ neurotic ♦ prospect ♦ share

a People are in ....when they are peaceful and agree with each other.

b Someone who worries all the time is often called ....

c We often use the phrase '...................................' to describe something that is clear and simple.

d When we expect something to happen, we say that there is a .... of it happening.

e When someone makes a .... on something, they decide what they think about it.

f A .... is a phrase that is repeated so often that we don't think about its meaning, such as 'blind as a bat' or 'raining buckets'.

g When two people .... something, they experience it together.

h When we .... things, we make them less clear and simple.

i When you always need the support of another person, you are .... them.

j When someone offers you something for nothing, it's easy to .... of believing them.

14 Is each of the following statements *True* or *False*? Write *T* or *F* in the brackets.

a Bob Narindra suggests that many people don't know whether what they are feeling is really love.   [ ]

b He thinks that the love for a pet is the same as the love for a friend.   [ ]

c He says that people who are in love want to tell the person they're in love with about everything that has happened to them.   [ ]

d He thinks that people who are in love can read each other's minds.   [ ]

e He suggests that you have to love others in order to be able to love yourself.   [ ]

f He warns that agreeing with anything the other person says is a sign of being too dependent on that person.   [ ]

g He is sure how to answer the question 'Is this love?'.   [ ]

h I think Bob Narindra gives good advice!   [ ]

Writing: 'small ads'

15 Match the abbreviations and words in the left-hand column with their meanings in the right-hand column.

a Call	Would like to meet
b GSOH	Please ring
c LTR	Good sense of humour
d Tel	Long-term relationship
e TLC	telephone number
f WLTM	Tender loving care

16 Look at the information and the example advertisement. Write advertisements for the next three people using as few words as possible. Abbreviations (such as *GSOH*) only count as one word.

a

I'm 26 years old and a primary teacher. I've got a good sense of humour. I want someone who likes dance music, and the cinema. I'm looking for a friend more than anything.

b

CRUME ENGINEERING

Here at Crume we're looking for a catering assistant. They must be pleasant and quick-thinking. We'll pay £140 a week. The phone number is 07888 444 5273 and the applicant needs to talk to me (Sandy).

c

DAY CARE CENTRE

We want a young person to help our work with disabled people on our summer camp. Applicants should be caring, kind, efficient and hardworking. We can agree on the pay when we meet them. Our phone number is 04527 45610.

d

I'm 32 years old. I drive a coach for a travel company. I like classical music, art, the theatre and walking. I want to meet someone who likes those things for tender loving care or a long-term relationship.

Advertisement text *a*	Advertisement text *b*	Advertisement text *c*	Advertisement text *d*
Male primary teacher, 26, with GSOH, WLTM someone who likes dance music and cinema for friendship.			

Pronunciation

17 Listen to Track 43. How do the people sound. Are they *Enthusiastic*, *Neutral* or *Unenthusiastic*? Write *E*, *N*, or *U* in the brackets.

a Can I get you a drink? [ ]
b Fantastic. [ ]
c He's asked me to the cinema. [ ]
d Hello Martin. [ ]
e How nice to hear from you. [ ]
f I'd love to. [ ]
g I'll have a coffee. [ ]
h I've got a new job. [ ]
i That would be great. [ ]
j Would you like to come to the cinema? [ ]

18 Listen to Track 43 again and repeat the phrases, sentences and questions, in the same way as the speakers.

REFLECTIONS

Thinking about learning and language: review of *Just Right (Intermediate)*

19 Complete the following table about *Just Right* (*Intermediate*).

What I enjoyed most in
Just Right (*Intermediate*) and why:

The most important thing I
have learnt since starting
Just Right (*Intermediate*):

The things I found most
difficult in *Just Right* (*Intermediate*):

The thing(s) I enjoyed least
about *Just Right* (*Intermediate*) and why:

20 Copy and complete this table by assessing your strengths and weaknesses in the various areas in the table. Write what you can do/what you know, write what problems you still have, and think about how you might continue learning now that you have finished *Just Right* (*Intermediate*).

Areas	I can/I know:	I still have trouble with:	My learning plan for this area, from now on, is:
Vocabulary			
Grammar			
Functional language			
Pronunciation			
Speaking			
Writing			
Listening			
Reading			

Test your knowledge

21 Which of the following statements and questions are correct? Put a tick (✓) or a cross (✗) in the brackets.

a He said he comes tomorrow. [ ]
b She asked she could see me again. [ ]
c He said he'd ring me in two days. [ ]
d They asked me what is my name. [ ]
e Carl talked a lot to Danuta at the party. [ ]
f They did not get on well together. [ ]
g He told me not to waste me time. [ ]
h It's not one of your business. [ ]
i I was wondering if you would like to come to the cinema. [ ]
j Do you fancy coming to the cinema? [ ]

Rewrite the items you marked with a cross, to make correct sentences.

The phonemic alphabet

22 Consult the table of phonemic symbols on page 123 and then write these words and phrases in ordinary spelling.

a /əˈkweɪntəns/ ....

b /ˈenəmɪ/ ....

c /nəˈgəʊʃəbəl/ ....

d /məˈkænɪk/ ....

e /ˌreɪtsəvˈpeɪ/ ....

f /nʌnəvjɔːˈbɪznɪs/ ....

g /aɪmiːzɪtəˈpliːz/

....

Check your answers by listening to Track 44.

Audioscript

TRACK 1

INTERVIEWER: Why did you leave your last job, Miss Franklin?

MISS FRANKLIN: Because they asked me to work too hard. I had to be there all the time from early in the morning to late at night. I had no life of my own. It was terrible. I hated it.

INTERVIEWER: Yes, it must have been very difficult.

MISS FRANKLIN: It was. I mean I know I have to work to earn money, but work isn't everything. Is it?

INTERVIEWER: Perhaps not. Are you a hard worker?

MISS FRANKLIN: Oh yes, I think so. I mean not all the time, but I am when I have to be.

INTERVIEWER: And can you work on your own?

MISS FRANKLIN: Yes, I think so. I'm not really sure.

INTERVIEWER: Miss Franklin, what do you do when you're not working?

MISS FRANKLIN: Go out with my friends. Go clubbing, you know to night clubs, dancing, that kind of thing.

INTERVIEWER: Do you have any hobbies?

MISS FRANKLIN: Well yes. Going out. Clubbing.

INTERVIEWER: Just clubbing?

MISS FRANKLIN: Well yes, I'm very keen on it.

INTERVIEWER: Why do you want this job, Miss Franklin?

MISS FRANKLIN: Because I need a change. Because I don't want to work too hard. Because the pay is good. Because my boyfriend works here.

INTERVIEWER: Ah yes. I see. That's Mr Adams, isn't it?

MISS FRANKLIN: Yes, that's him.

INTERVIEWER: And what has he told you about our company?

MISS FRANKLIN: Just good things, really. That it's a nice place to work. You're all great people. Good atmosphere. That kind of thing.

INTERVIEWER: That's what he's told you.

MISS FRANKLIN: Yes. Well, most of it anyway.

INTERVIEWER: We're running out of time here. Do you have any questions for us?

MISS FRANKLIN: Er, yes. Just one. Will I be left on my own a lot?

INTERVIEWER: Oh no. We'll keep an eye on you, see how you're getting on.

INTERVIEWER: That's if you get the job.

MISS FRANKLIN: OK. Thanks.

INTERVIEWER: Anything else?

MISS FRANKLIN: No, thank you.

INTERVIEWER: All right then. We'll let you know.

MISS FRANKLIN: OK...er.....thanks. Goodbye.

INTERVIEWER: Goodbye.

Track 2

a What do you think of Lisa?

b What do you do in advertising?

c Have you two met before?

d How long have you known Ruth?

e Can I ask you a question?

f Do you enjoy studying zoology?

g What time is your taxi coming?

Track 3

a assertive

b loyal

c unkind

d sincere

e indecisive

f considerate

Track 4

PETER: ... they will just have to start talking if they want the peace process to continue. And now back to you, Jim, in the studio in London.

JIM: Well, that was Peter Janus reporting from the United Nations. Now for our next piece we're going over to Sue Ballot in Vaness, north-west France, with an incredible story of survival.

SUE: Yes Jim, and it is an incredible story. Yesterday, a married couple, Kevin McIlwee and his wife Beverly, both of them from the island of Jersey, had a miraculous escape after plunging 10,000 feet when their parachutes failed to open properly. They broke a number of bones, but amazingly they're still alive.

I should explain that Kevin (he's 47) and Beverly (just three years younger) were on their honeymoon. Mr McIlwee is a parachute instructor, and persuaded his new wife to do a tandem jump – that's when an instructor jumps with someone (in this case Beverly) strapped to him.

The accident happened when the first parachute didn't open properly. Mr McIlwee tried to solve the problem, but when he couldn't, he tried to get rid of that chute and use the second emergency parachute that skydivers always carry with them.

A few hours ago I spoke to Beverly's father, Dennis Murtaugh, who explained what happened next. His words were spoken by an actor because the line was not good when we talked.

DENNIS: Unfortunately, Kevin wasn't able to jettison the first parachute properly, so the emergency chute wouldn't open and they just fell faster and faster. Kevin told me that they thought that was it, they were going to die.

SUE: So how did they survive?

DENNIS: It was pure luck, I suppose. I mean they only had half a parachute to slow them down. They hit the ground at an absolutely fantastic speed. It could have killed them.

SUE: How does your daughter feel about parachuting now?

DENNIS: She's never going to do another jump!

SUE: I'm not surprised.

DENNIS: She's only just starting to realise how lucky she is. When I spoke to her she said she was looking out of the window from her hospital bed enjoying seeing the daylight and the birds.

SUE: Beverly McIlwee needs a number of operations and will be in a wheelchair for weeks. She has broken bones in her leg, ankle and both of her feet. Her husband has a broken leg. Jim?

JIM: Thanks very much for that report Sue. Well, that's a honeymoon those two people will never forget! And now it's time for sport, so over to Simon …

Track 5

a He's rather interesting.
b I was pretty scared.
c It was absolutely amazing.
d It was absolutely hilarious.
e She was rather angry.
f They're really good.
g Your room's absolutely filthy.

Track 6

a amazing
b conscious
c hilarious
d pretty amazing
e remembered
f sure
g unconscious

Track 7

WOMAN: Excuse me, sir.

MAN: Yes. What?

WOMAN: Can you give me just a few minutes of your time?

MAN: It's not very convenient. I'm in a bit of a hurry.

WOMAN: It'll only take a second.

MAN: A second. I don't think so.

WOMAN: OK, then a couple of minutes.

MAN: Look, I'm really busy. I don't think …

WOMAN: Oh please, sir. If you answer just a few questions you'll automatically be entered into our prize draw.

MAN: Sorry?

WOMAN: Our prize draw. Everyone who takes part in this survey is entered into our prize draw, which takes place in three weeks.

MAN: What's the prize?

WOMAN: A holiday for two in Jamaica.

MAN: What are my chances of winning?

WOMAN: The same as anybody else's, I suppose.

MAN: How many people are taking part in this survey?

WOMAN: I wouldn't know.

MAN: Look, this is really …

WOMAN: Come on sir, you've spent a couple of minutes talking to me already. You might as well answer a few questions.

MAN: Oh all right, if you must. But let's get a move on.

WOMAN: Right, well the first question is 'How often do you go shopping? Once a week, twice a week, three times a week or more than three times a week?'

MAN: Oh, once a week – but only if I have to!

WOMAN: Yes … and how many items do you usually buy when you go shopping: one, two, between three and five, between six and ten or more than ten?

MAN: I don't know, really. I suppose, well, usually it's a couple of things. No more than two anyway.

WOMAN: I'll put two then. The next question is 'How much time do you spend when you go shopping, an hour …'

MAN: I don't understand the question.

WOMAN: Well, when you go shopping how long do you spend for the whole expedition? Less than an hour, between one and two hours or more than two hours?

MAN: Oh. less than an hour, if possible. I mean it's not something I do for fun!

WOMAN: OK, the fourth question, 'When you go shopping for clothes what do you buy most often, trousers, shirts, underwear, T-shirts, jackets or sweaters?'

MAN: I've absolutely no idea.

WOMAN: Well just say one of them, any one.

MAN: Any one?

WOMAN: Yes. Why not?

MAN: All right. Trousers.

WOMAN: Right. The last question, 'What is your favourite colour for a pair of trousers?'

MAN: Never thought about it.

WOMAN: Yes but if you did?

MAN: Black, I suppose.

WOMAN: Right, well that's it. Now if you'd just like to write your name and address here, your name will go forward for the prize.

MAN: The holiday in Jamaica.

WOMAN: Yes! If you're lucky, you'll be flying to Jamaica.

MAN: I won't be. I never am.

WOMAN: Don't be so pessimistic. You never know.

MAN: Oh yes I do. I never win anything!

Track 8

a There's a nice stall in the market.
  There're nice stalls in the market.

b Very few people eat meat.
  Very few people eat meat.

c I'll do the late-night shopping on Friday.
  I do the late-night shopping on Friday.

d It makes me feel angry.
  It makes me feel hungry.

e Can I help you?
  Can I help you?

f I'm looking for a fleece.
  I'm looking for the police.

Track 9

a fleece
b expedition
c serious
d supermarket
e anything
f several
g vacuum-packed

Track 10

1

This is the last call for flight BA two four oh nine to Bogotá. Would all the remaining passengers on this flight please proceed to gate number 35 as this plane is now boarding.

2

Here is a platform announcement. The 6.52 to Kings Lynn will now depart from platform 4 and not from platform 1. Kings Lynn, platform 4.

3

Good morning, ladies and gentlemen. We're now ready to board the aircraft, flight BA two four oh nine to Bogotá. Could all passengers in rows 20 to 39 please come to the desk with their boarding cards and passports. Thank you very much.

4

West Anglia regrets to announce the delay of the 12.35 to London King's Cross. This train is running approximately 15, one five, minutes late.

5

Good afternoon ladies and gentlemen. Sorry for the delay. A train has broken down in front of us so we can't proceed, but they've told me they're working on it so we shouldn't be here for too long.

6

We will shortly be landing at Manchester airport. The captain has switched on the seatbelt sign so will all passengers please return to your seats, fasten your seat belts, fold your trays into the back of the seat in front of you and place your seats in the upright position.

7

Welcome to Manchester airport. For your own safety please keep your seatbelts fastened until the plane reaches the terminal building and the captain has switched off the seatbelt sign.

Track 11

a That ship is really big.
b Phew! It's very hot in here.
c I don't like the noise that sheep make.
d This is a nice place.
e It's a really good club.
f After two weeks on holiday I feel fat.
g The weather's better this week, isn't it?
h What's the plan for tomorrow?
i I always choose holidays in the sun.
j Excuse me, that's my seat.

Track 12

a sightseeing
b package holiday
c water skiing
d Backpackerland
e exotic
f uncomfortable
g off the beaten track

Track 13

AGENT: Come on in and have a look around.

PAUL: Thanks.

AGENT: OK, so this is the kitchen.

HILARY: It's a bit cramped, isn't it?

AGENT: Yes, but look at the view.

PAUL: Yes, Hilary, that is pretty fantastic.

HILARY: Yes, I suppose so.

AGENT: OK, if you've seen enough here, let's go through into the living room.

HILARY: It's very cold here. Is it always this cold?

AGENT: Well, the house has been empty for the last seven months. The last tenants moved out in a hurry.

PAUL: Why?

AGENT: We don't know. They just said they didn't like it any more. They left just like that. As if they were running away.

HILARY: Perhaps it was because of the cold.

AGENT: Oh no. The owners have had central heating put in – it's not on at the moment. Look, here in the living room there's a big fireplace.

PAUL: Oh, this is great. So light, really spacious. Don't you think so Hilary?

HILARY: Yes, it's lovely. What's the upstairs like?

AGENT: Come and see.

AGENT: Here we are. Here's the main bedroom.

PAUL: Oh yes. That's amazing. Just imagine waking up to that view. Every morning. I love this old cupboard.

AGENT: And if you'd like to come along here, you can see the second bedroom.

PAUL: Hilary! This is perfect. Small, just the right size. I can put a table in here. Yes, I can write in this room.

AGENT: You're a writer?

PAUL: Yes, that's why we want a house out here in the country. I'm finishing a novel.

AGENT: Have you had anything published?

PAUL: Well no, not yet, actually. But it's only a matter of time.

AGENT: And what do you do, madam?

HILARY: Well, I'm an actor. But I'm having a few months' rest at the moment.

AGENT: Interesting. Have I seen you in anything?

HILARY: Probably not. Most of my work is in radio.

AGENT: OK, so this is the bathroom.

HILARY: It doesn't have any windows.

PAUL: Yes, but that doesn't matter, love. I mean this house is perfect. No television, no telephone. I'm really going to like it here.

AGENT: So, you've decided?

PAUL: Yes.

HILARY: Can't we talk about it first?

PAUL: Nothing to talk about. We'll take it. For six months.

Track 14

a It's great to see you.

b Oh, this is great!

c Can I take your coat?

d It's a bit cramped in here.

e I've just won a prize.

f Can I get you something to drink?

g Thanks for inviting us.

Track 15

a homeless

b spacious

c bungalow

d garage

e the open air

f block of flats

g Thanks for coming.

Track 16

JANE: So, do you like living here, Hilary?

HILARY: Yes. It's a great place to rent while Paul is writing his novel. But I wouldn't like to live here for ever.

PAUL: It's got ghosts, apparently.

MARK: Oh don't be silly. Nobody believes in ghosts.

PAUL: Why not, Mark?

MARK: Oh, Paul! You're a rational human being. You can't believe all that stuff.

JANE: What's the story, then, about this place? Why does it have ghosts?

HILARY: Well apparently, Jane, about 300 years ago a family lived here. Mother, father, two kids. And one night …

PAUL: Terrible weather, wind, rain …

MARK: A night like this you mean?

HILARY: Yes, I suppose so, anyway there was a knock at the door, two men outside. They said 'Please can we stay the night.' They were cold and hungry. So they were given food and somewhere to sleep.

PAUL: But that night the whole family was murdered and the two strangers were never seen again.

HILARY: And that's why, on cold winter nights you can hear the family cry 'strangers, strangers' and sometimes they even …

JANE: What was that?

PAUL: Oh no! Not again. The electricity. I wonder how long we'll be without light this time.

MARK: Do you have any candles?

HILARY: Not sure. Have we got any left?

PAUL: I think so. I know where they are. I'll go.

HILARY: Thanks, Paul.

JANE: What was that?

HILARY: What was what?

JANE: That noise.

HILARY: I didn't hear a noise.

JANE: There. Listen.

MARK: Oh come on love, you're being silly.

JANE: I'm really cold. Anyone else cold?

HILARY: Yes. Suddenly … it's suddenly cold.

GHOSTLY VOICE: Strangers in the house … strangers in the house.

JANE: Did you hear that?

MARK: It's just Paul playing around. Paul? Paul?

JANE: Oh my God, what was that?

MARK: It's OK, leave this to me. I'll go and see.

HILARY: No Mark, stay here.

MARK: It's OK. Back in a minute.

JANE: I don't like this, Hilary.

HILARY: No, neither do I.

JANE: Paul? Mark? Paul? Mark?

HILARY: I hate being in the dark like this. Can't see anything ... I ... it's ... Oh no ...

JANE: Hilary. Hilary. Hilary. Hilary …

Track 17

a She inherited a million dollars?

b She inherited a million dollars.

c A million dollars.

d A million dollars?

e You like spaghetti?

f You like spaghetti.

g Yes.

h Yes?

i He was given a prize?

j He was given a prize.

k They really suit me.

l They really suit me?

Track 18

a conquered

b executed

c disguised

d corduroy

e leather

f How interesting.

g I dunno. (don't know)

Track 19

CHARLIE: And now, at five past eight here on Breakfast Television, it's time for our weather report from Samantha Sweet. Good morning, Sam.

SAM: Hello Charlie, and good morning to all of you watching.

As usual, everything depends on where you live this morning. Some of you will be luckier than others. We've got everything: rain, heavy snowfall, freezing conditions, but sunshine too.

Right, so let's start with the south-west of the country. As you can see from the chart, it's started quite cold – about 3 degrees centigrade – but it'll warm up as the day goes on, reaching about eight degrees by the afternoon. It's going to be cloudy with sunny periods, I think, but it's going to be a cold night, though, down below freezing – about minus 1, I should think. So be warned!

In the south-east, things are much the same, though not quite as warm as in the south-west. But I don't expect temperatures to fall below freezing tonight. That's because of a warmer breeze coming in from the Channel.

In the middle of the country, things are a bit more confused. Right now it's about 5 degrees centigrade, cloudy, and with some light rain. But that situation is going to change as the day goes on, and by the end of the day it will probably be raining quite heavily and the rain will continue through the night, only easing up tomorrow morning. But don't expect much dry weather in the next few days.

Things aren't quite so bad in Wales and the west. Here the rain will gradually die away in the late afternoon, so people can expect quite a dry night, though tomorrow looks like being a day of scattered showers.

Up the east coast of the country, in the north, and further north into Scotland, it's pretty cold already, as anyone there knows. It's about minus 2 degrees centigrade, with heavy cloud, but that should go up to about 1 degree during the morning. But the outlook doesn't look good. Expect some snow by midday, starting quite light, but gradually increasing so that by the evening it will be heavy, with blizzard-like conditions on the road, so do be careful. In fact the police have just issued advice to motorists not to travel at all unless their journey is absolutely necessary. Temperatures tonight will drop to about minus 6 degrees.

And what of tomorrow? As I said, in the middle of the country, it's going to be wet and cloudy, scattered showers with the occasional burst of heavier rainfall. In the north and east, people should settle in for a cold spell with more snowfall over the next few days. Not quite so bad in the south and west, though. Here there will be some sunshine – when it isn't raining, that is.

And that's the end of this morning's forecast. Charlie?

CHARLIE: Thanks, Sam. By the way, you won't be worried about the weather for the next few days, will you?

SAM: No, Charlie, I won't. I'm off on holiday to the sunny Caribbean this afternoon for ten days.

CHARLIE: Well have a nice time, Sam. We'll miss you. And now back to our main news story this morning. The prime minister has announced …

Track 20

a I <u>promise</u> I'll be at your house by four o'clock.
b I promise I'll be at your house by <u>four o'clock</u>.
c I promise I'll be at your <u>house</u> by four o'clock.
d I promise <u>I'll</u> be at your house by four o'clock.
e I promise I'll be at <u>your</u> house by four o'clock.

Track 21

a tomorrow
b wedding
c resolution
d firefighter
e New Year's Eve
f Nobody's perfect.
g I can't cope.

Track 22

1

MAN: Excuse me. … Excuse me.
YOUNG WOMAN: Sorry? What's the problem?
MAN: Could you turn that thing off?
YOUNG WOMAN: Sorry? What was that?
MAN: Listen, take your headphones off!
YOUNG WOMAN: Sorry?
MAN: Take your headphones off!
YOUNG WOMAN: All right, all right.
MAN: Listen, I can't stand your machine. Ticka ticka ticka all the time. It's driving me mad.
YOUNG WOMAN: All right, all right. I'll go and sit somewhere else.
MAN: Yes, why don't you do that.
YOUNG WOMAN: Cor! Crazy old fool.

2

MAN 1: Hey you!
CYCLIST: Sorry? What?
MAN 1: Stop! Stop!
CYCLIST: Why, what's the matter?
MAN 1: Can't you read the sign?
CYCLIST: What sign?
MAN 1: Look. It means you can't ride on the pavement.
CYCLIST: Oh. Oh well, I didn't see it.
MAN 1: Well you've seen it now, OK?
CYCLIST: Yeah, I suppose so.

3

POLICEWOMAN: Excuse me, sir.
MAN: Yes? What's the problem Officer?
POLICEWOMAN: Have you just eaten some crisps?
MAN: Yes, why?
POLICEWOMAN: And drunk a cola?
MAN: Yes. But I don't see …
POLICEWOMAN: And you left the packet and the can on the grass.
MAN: Did I …? Oh.
POLICEWOMAN: Yes, and that sign? What does that sign mean?
MAN: It means you mustn't drop litter, I suppose.
POLICEWOMAN: That's correct, sir. So what are you going to do?
MAN: I think I'm going to pick the packet and the can up.
POLICEWOMAN: That's exactly what I think, sir. Now isn't that a coincidence!

4

MAN: And so I said to Martin, well, if you're going to be like that … what … Oh … well … I'm on the train … yes, well Martin said that the foreign …
WOMAN: I can't stand this. I really can't.
DAUGHTER: Oh Mum, leave it out.
WOMAN: No, I'm going to say something!
DAUGHTER: Why?
WOMAN: Because I don't want to have to listen to his conversation. It's driving me crazy!
MAN: … well, of course, Martin was completely amazed because I was right, I mean, I don't want to boast or anything …
WOMAN: Excuse me!
MAN: … but I am cleverer than Martin.
WOMAN: Will you please be quiet. Just be quiet! I can't stand it any more.
MAN: Er … what? … Nothing, mate, nothing … Listen … got to go. Bye.
WOMAN: Well, thank you.
DAUGHTER: Oh Mum!

Track 23

amazing, certainly, exactly, forbidden, graffiti, occasion, opinion, permission, sensitive, signature

Track 24

a It is six o'clock, here is the news…
b Last call for passengers on…
c Welcome to the ABC cinema automated booking system…
d Excuse me, can you tell me the way to the university?
e Here is a staff announcement…
f So I'd like you to give a warm welcome to Dr Stella Cross who is going to talk to us about body language. Dr Cross …
g Who goes there?
h Good morning everybody. Now before we start …

Track 25

a precinct
b litter
c car alarm
d policy
e graffiti
f strictly forbidden
g Help yourself.

Track 26

a

ACTOR: How do I play this scene?
DIRECTOR: It's difficult to say. I think you're probably quite angry in this bit.
ACTOR: OK, so what do you recommend?
DIRECTOR: I think you can come in and shake your fist at Caspar as you start talking.
ACTOR: Anything else?
DIRECTOR: Well, you could fold your arms then so that you go on looking angry.
ACTOR: Is this what you had in mind?
DIRECTOR: Yes, that's the type of thing.

b

ACTOR: How do you want me to do this scene?
DIRECTOR: That's not easy to say. My impression is that you're probably a bit bored in this scene.
ACTOR: OK. So what do I do?
DIRECTOR: Well, I think you can show boredom by folding your arms, or crossing your legs when you sit down.
ACTOR: Is that all?

DIRECTOR: Well, you could shrug your shoulders when she talks to you.
ACTOR: Like this?
DIRECTOR: Yes, that's the kind of thing.

Track 27

The way you wear your hat
The way you sip your tea
The memory of all that
No, no, they can't take that away from me.

The way your smile just beams
The way you sing off-key
The way you haunt my dreams
No, no, they can't take that away from me.

We may never, never meet again on the bumpy road to love
Still I'll always, always keep the memory of

The way you hold your knife
The way we danced till three
The way you changed my life
No, no they can't take that away from me.
No, they can't take that away from me.

The way your smile just beams
The way you sing off-key
The way you haunt my dreams
No, they can't take that away from me.

We may never, never meet again on the bumpy road to love
Still I'll always, always keep the memory of

The way you hold your knife
The way we danced till three
The way you changed my life
No, no they can't take that away from me
No, they can't take that away from me.

Track 28

1 Stop biting your nails!
2 I'm pleased to see you.
3 Don't shake your fist at me!
4 I am telling the truth.
5 It's so nice to see you.
6 Are you waving at me?
7 Don't raise your eyebrows at me!
8 I quite agree with you.

Track 29

a eyebrow
b shoulder
c scratching
d witness
e tell the truth
f telling the truth
g face-to-face

Track 30

TOM: What do you want to study at university?

MICHELLE: Science.

TOM: Science?!

MICHELLE: Yes. I'm going to do combined chemistry and physics. What's wrong with that?

TOM: Well, I don't know. It's … it's just that, well, science!

MICHELLE: Sorry?

TOM: Well, I mean half the world's problems are because of science.

MICHELLE: Come again?

TOM: No look, I'm serious, I mean what have scientists ever done for us?

MICHELLE: What, you mean apart from giving us cars.

TOM: Well yes, apart from giving us cars …

MICHELLE: And aeroplanes.

TOM: OK, cars and aeroplanes, I agree, but look what they're doing to the planet: all that contamination, all that pollution, and you can't get anywhere because you get stuck in traffic jams …

MICHELLE: And don't forget the computer.

TOM: All right, all right, I agree, science has given us the computer too, but that's not so special, is it? I mean there are people all over the world who can't get anywhere near a computer. Anyway, they always crash.

MICHELLE: Oh, you're just being ridiculous!

TOM: Look, I accept that science has given us cars and planes and the computer, all right. But apart from them, what have scientists ever really done for us?

MICHELLE: What about medicine?

TOM: What about medicine?

MICHELLE: Well, without science and scientists most children wouldn't survive for more than about five years, and if we did make it into adulthood we'd all be dead before we were 50.

TOM: Well, I …

MICHELLE: Just think of all the drugs that keep people alive, all of them discovered by scientists. Think of the aspirin you take for a headache, the antibiotics that cure infections, all of those things.

TOM: Well, if science is so wonderful, how come we still don't know how to cure the common cold?

MICHELLE: Look, just …

TOM: And as for antibiotics, people have taken so many antibiotics that they don't work any more. There are new illnesses that are drug-resistant.

MICHELLE: Oh yes, but who will find out how to get round that problem?

TOM: I haven't the slightest idea.

MICHELLE: Scientists, of course. 'What have scientists ever done for us?' What a stupid question.

TOM: It's not.

MICHELLE: Anyway, what are you going to study?

TOM: Film studies.

MICHELLE: Film studies?!

TOM: Yes. Why not?

MICHELLE: Oh come on. You can't be serious. I mean what have film makers ever done for us?

TOM: What, apart from making us laugh?

MICHELLE: Well yes, apart from making us laugh …

TOM: And making us cry.

MICHELLE: Yes, yes, I agree, and making us cry. Big deal! What's special about that? Anyway apart from laughing and crying, what have film makers ever done for us?

Track 31

a <u>Thank</u> you.
b Thank <u>you</u>.
c Thanks a <u>lot</u>.
d Thank you <u>very</u> much.
e Thank you <u>very</u> <u>much</u> for your <u>help</u>.
f <u>No</u> problem.
g Don't <u>ment</u>ion it.
h <u>Glad</u> I could <u>help</u>.

Track 32

a calculator
b monitor
c television
d proficient
e computer virus
f out of date
g Can you help me?

Track 33

Conversation 1

MAN: What do you think of that?

WOMAN: It's absolutely wonderful!

MAN: Look at that girl in the background … the way the sunlight catches her hair …

WOMAN: Yes, it's lovely.

MAN: ... and all the farm workers in the foreground. They're so realistic. It's just so full of life.

WOMAN: Yes, it's wonderful. Now let's talk about something else.

Conversation 2

WOMAN: Look at that. Isn't it fantastic!

MAN: Is it?

WOMAN: Don't you think so?

MAN: Not really. Not my kind of thing at all.

WOMAN: Oh come on. Look at that girl in the background.

MAN: What about her?

WOMAN: The sunlight on her hair. Magical.

MAN: So what. She doesn't look like a real person at all. And all these people in the foreground, they're supposed to be musicians, are they?

WOMAN: It's art, Paul.

MAN: Well, perhaps I just don't like art!

Conversation 3

TEENAGER 1: Wow!

TEENAGER 2: Yeah.

TEENAGER 1: I mean, was that frightening or what?

TEENAGER 2: You're right. It was frightening. Absolutely terrifying. I was, like, so scared.

TEENAGER 1: Me too. I could hardly watch most of the time.

TEENAGER 2: Shall we see it again?

TEENAGER 1: Yes, yes, let's. It was so good.

TEENAGER 2: Brilliant!

Conversation 4

MAN 1: Did you enjoy that?

MAN 2: Of course I did. I absolutely loved it.

MAN 1: You didn't think it was a bit, you know, silly?

MAN 2: Silly? No. It was really good fun. I couldn't stop laughing.

MAN 1: I know. You laugh really loudly, you know.

MAN 2: Do I?

MAN 1: Yes, you do.

MAN 2: Well you hardly laughed at all.

MAN 1: I didn't think it was that funny.

MAN 2: You just don't have a sense of humour!

MAN 1: Well, thanks.

Conversation 5

WOMAN 1: Well, did you enjoy that?

WOMAN 2: Yes, of course. But it was pretty frightening, wasn't it?

WOMAN 1: That was half the fun!

WOMAN 2: Right. You know what was amazing?

WOMAN 1: No, what?

WOMAN 2: Well, we hardly ever actually saw the lady herself, did we? In fact, I'm not even sure if we did. But it was still pretty scary!

WOMAN 1: Yes, it was quite alarming once or twice.

WOMAN 2: You know what I think.

WOMAN 1: No, what?

WOMAN 2: There's nothing better than a good piece of live theatre.

WOMAN 1: Yes, you're probably right.

Track 34

a You might have <u>hurt</u> yourself.

b You can't have been very <u>pleased</u>.

c That must have been <u>terrifying</u>.

d You could have been in <u>real</u> danger.

e That couldn't have been <u>plea</u>sant.

Track 35

a art

b foreground

c sculpture

d autobiography

e controversy

f wonderful

g It doesn't matter.

Track 36

TV COMMENTATOR 1: What a fantastic game! The atmosphere is absolutely electric, and with the score at one all it looks like we'll have to go into extra time and then, well, who knows what may happen. That's the thing about extra time, you never ...

TV COMMENTATOR 2: Yes, but it's not over yet. Liverpool are really putting on the pressure ...

ANGELA: Could you answer the phone, love?

GEOFF: I can't. You get it. I'm watching the game. There's only a few minutes left.

ANGELA: Geoff, please. I'm cooking. My hands are all messy.

GEOFF: Oh, all right. I suppose so. Hello? Oh hello Mum ... watching the football. Arsenal against Liverpool ... What? ... Yes, it's nearly finished ... Have you? You've seen a new car you want to buy? ... Well, I'm sure you can get a different colour. Look Mum, can I ring you back? ... Yes, of course I want to speak to you ... no, no, please don't be upset ... I just want to watch the end of this game. You know how important it is ... yes, I promise. In about five minutes or so.

ANGELA: Who was that?

GEOFF: My mother.

ANGELA: What did she want?

GEOFF: Tell you later.

GEOFF: Oh no. Not again.

ANGELA: Geoff!

GEOFF: All right, all right. Hello … Hello, Clive … you're feeling unhappy, are you? … Well, if she doesn't want to go out with you, I would stop ringing her. But look, can I ring you back? It's the Cup Final … I know you're my brother … Yes, yes, I do care about you. But I'll ring you back … because I don't want to talk to you right now. Goodbye.

ANGELA: Geoff?

GEOFF: Yes, what?

ANGELA: Can you just come here and help me? I can't open this tin.

GEOFF: Not now, Angela.

ANGELA: Oh please. If I don't get this thing open, we won't have any dinner.

GEOFF: But there's only a couple of minutes left, and if Liverpool score again.

ANGELA: Geoff! Please.

GEOFF: Oh all right. If I must … Show me the tin. Come on. I haven't got much time …

TV COMMENTATOR 2: … and he's through the defenders, there's only the goalkeeper and he's past him so surely … yes, goal! Goal! What a fantastic goal! And the crowd are on their feet …

GEOFF: What? What? Oh no! They've scored. They've scored and I didn't see it.

ANGELA: Who's scored?

GEOFF: Liverpool. It's two one. They've almost certainly won the game.

ANGELA: Well, that's good, isn't it?

GEOFF: Well, of course it is, but I didn't see it.

ANGELA: Well, you can watch the – what do they call it – replay, surely.

GEOFF: Yes, but it's not the same … it's just not … oh what's the point!

ANGELA: Come on, Geoff, it's only a football game!

Track 37

a Ow! My shoulder hurts.

b Look at his toes! They're broken.

c If I was you, I'd give it to him.

d If you rang home now, it would be all right.

e If you do this work for me, I'll give you three tickets.

Track 38

a defender

b injury

c referee

d broken toe

e stomach-ache

f training session

g under the weather

Track 39

CAROL: I started playing the cello when I was about eight or nine – I can't remember actually – and I kept on with it for quite a few years. I used to practise quite a lot and there was a time when I didn't mind doing it at all. It was great playing the cello because I was in youth orchestras, that kind of thing, and we went abroad to do tours. I've still got some really good friends I made in those orchestras, and we had some really good times on our trips – though I think we were quite a handful for the poor adults who had to look after us. But anyway when I got to university I stopped playing. Well, there just wasn't time and there were so many other things to do. So I haven't actually taken the instrument out of the case for ages now!

I really used to enjoy playing. I'll go back to it some day, I hope. I think it's like riding a bicycle. You know, you never forget once you've learned.

DANIEL: My father plays the saxophone, he's absolutely crazy about jazz. He's always playing or listening to jazz records. My mum complains sometimes! She says he spends more time on his music than on his job.

When I was little I thought I'd end up learning the sax too, but then decided that I sort of wanted to have my own instrument so instead of the saxophone I chose the trumpet. I've been learning for about five years now, and I love it. I'm in the school jazz band. We get to play at school concerts and things. I'm really into jazz; it's just great. I'd like to be a professional musician when I grow up but my dad says it's difficult to earn a living from music. But I so don't want to be a lawyer like him. It's just like so boring.

CARMEN: Nobody likes living near someone like me because when I practise I make a lot of noise! But you have to keep practising don't you, otherwise it gets more and more difficult. Trouble is, in the summer, when it's hot, I have to open the windows, so the whole street gets to hear if I'm not careful. I love playing drums, I love the whole drum kit. You can make so many different sounds, so many different rhythms. Sometimes I just play on my own for hours and hours.

Drummers are special! We keep the band together, see, it's our rhythm that really matters. Of course you have to have a good bass guitarist too, and if the rest of the group are, well, not up to it, it doesn't really matter what you do. But I play in a fantastic band so that's fine.

I enjoy playing jazz – I play in a big band sometimes - but it's rock music that I like best. When you get a really good driving beat, there's nothing like it. The power. And it's a very physical thing too. You stay pretty fit if you're a drummer!

VINCE: I've played guitar and sung folk songs for as long as I can remember. I'm not sure how it started really, though my mother says she gave me my first guitar and taught me a few chords. But anyway, after school, when I was trying to make it as a musician, I used to busk in the Underground in London to earn a bit of extra money. I took my guitar abroad with me too and I'd sing in cafés to pay for my holidays.

I tried to get a recording contract in those days, but in the end I couldn't find anyone who thought I was as good as I thought I was! So I kept on playing but I got a job as a waiter to pay my way. And then I got really interested in the restaurant business and now, well, I own three restaurants, as you know. But when I get any spare time – which isn't often – I still play. I've got a few friends who like folk music too. We have a sort of group. It's really good fun.

Track 40

1 Oh you poor thing.
2 It can't have been that bad.
3 That sounds terrible.
4 I made a real mess of it.
5 It could have been worse.
6 Oh good!
7 I think it went OK.
8 I couldn't think what to write.
9 I'm sure it wasn't as bad as you think.
10 Absolutely terrible.

Track 41

a cellist
b enjoy
c suggest
d photographer
e accompanist
f I'm out of here.
g I may as well go home.

Track 42

RADIO CONTINUITY: And now at five past twelve it's time for our morning story. Nick Ellis reads *Who your friends are* by Peter Hedley.

NICK ELLIS: The world's media arrived one hot summer's afternoon at about five thirty. Most of the neighbours had just come back from work. They had a ringside seat.

I still blame the TV crews and the cameramen. They could have just come quietly and knocked on the door, like anybody else, or rung me up for a comment. But they didn't. Their cars and TV vans roared down our street in the muggy heat. I heard them from the garden. Most of the neighbours must have been looking out of their windows even before the vehicles screeched to a halt and a large crowd of men and women clutching cameras, notepads and microphones jumped to the ground and headed for my house.

I had got up from the garden chair I was sitting in when I heard them hammering on my door. For a moment I couldn't decide what to do and then I thought, well, I may as well go and see what they want, so I walked towards the kitchen.

There was a loud crash behind me. I turned round. Two photographers had climbed over the wall and one of them had fallen on top of the dustbins. He started to yell and curse.

Up until that moment I had absolutely no idea what was going on. I had just been sitting in the sunshine with a cool orange juice wondering what I would do, now that I had left my job in a government research department. I had wanted to leave for some time. I didn't like the secrecy. I wanted to be able to talk about what I did to my friends. Oh all right, I'll admit it. It wasn't a research department, exactly, it was a secret department. The secret service actually. I can tell you that because it was in all the papers.

Anyway, I was just about to ask the two intruders at the back of the garden what they were doing when I heard footsteps in the house. I turned round again and my wife was running into the garden.

'I'm sorry,' she called, 'they were all here when I got back. I didn't mean to let them in. They just pushed their way past me. I couldn't help it.'

She was right. She couldn't. A whole crowd of people had pushed past her and were now surrounding me, cameras flashing, tape recorders whirring away.

'Is it true?' one of them shouted, 'are you the traitor?'

'Am I the what?' I asked. *Traitor* was not a word I liked. No one liked words like that in the secret service.

Now they were all shouting at once.

'Did you sell state secrets to the enemy?'

'How much did they pay you?'

'What's the matter, don't you love your country?'

'How well do you know Clem Mullen?'

'What?' I said; that last question worried me.

'How well do you get along with Clem Mullen? Is he a friend of yours or what?'

'Not really. We're acquaintances.'

'So you admit you know him!'

'Of course I do. I mean he's a ...' I was going to say colleague, but I'd left my job, and anyway you don't tell anyone about who you work with in the secret service - even if you don't know them very well.

It went on like this for days. They put my photograph in the papers, and there were pictures of me on the television news. There were pictures of Clem Mullen, too. But after a week or two they decided that I was nothing to do with it. They must have mixed me up with someone else. Gradually the media forgot about me and left me alone. But some people never really believed in my innocence. They thought I must be guilty, just like Clem Mullen. According to the police he <u>had</u> been selling secrets, but they have never been able to prove it because he just disappeared into thin air – and hasn't been seen to this day.

You soon find out who your real friends are in situations like that. The young woman next door, for example. She came round as soon as the newspapers and television had forgotten about me.

'You poor thing,' she said, 'it must have terrible for you.' And I said that it was, and my wife told her how difficult it had been for both of us.

The Revells, who live opposite, invited us over for a meal. They said how much they hated the media and how it was time someone stopped them 'doorstepping' innocent people – crowding round their front door steps and back gardens trying to get photographs and interviews. 'No one can live like that,' Mrs Revell said, and my wife agreed. She had nearly left the country because of it.

But the rest of them? They wouldn't even look at me. They still cross the street when they see me coming. 'No smoke without fire' they mutter darkly, and I think how unfair they are. Everyone is innocent until proved guilty. The police have never even been to question me. As far as they are concerned, I was just a victim of the press getting things wrong, badly wrong.

And I think - what would they say if I told them the truth?

Track 43

a Can I get you a drink?

b Fantastic.

c He's asked me to the cinema.

d Hello Martin.

e How nice to hear from you.

f I'd love to.

g I'll have a coffee.

h I've got a new job.

i That would be great.

j Would you like to come to the cinema?

Track 44

a acquaintance

b enemy

c negotiable

d mechanic

e rates of pay

f none of your business

g I'm easy to please.

Table of phonemic symbols

Consonants

Symbol	Example
p	please
b	better
t	truth
d	dark
k	class
g	go
f	finish
v	very
θ	thin
ð	that
s	sing
z	zoo
ʃ	shop
ʒ	measure
h	help
x	loch
tʃ	children
dʒ	join
m	some
n	son
ŋ	sing
w	wait
l	late
r	read
j	yes

Vowels

	Symbol	Example
short	ɪ	sit
	e	said
	æ	bat
	ɒ	top
	ʌ	luck
	ʊ	foot
	ə	again
long	iː	sleep
	aː	car
	ɔː	forward
	uː	school
	ɜː	heard
diphthongs	eɪ	lake
	aɪ	tie
	ɔɪ	joy
	əʊ	go
	aʊ	wow!
	ɪə	peculiar
	eə	air
	ʊə	cruel